BEAUTIFUL
THREADS

Other books by Mary Tatem

A Scrapbook of Life
The Quilt of Life
Just Call Me Mom

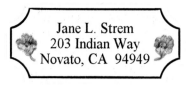

BEAUTIFUL THREADS

Pieces of Encouragement for Quilters

MARY TATEM

ILLUSTRATED BY KEVIN INGRAM

Fleming H. Revell

A Division of Baker Book House Co
Grand Rapids, Michigan 49516

Text © 2004 by Mary Tatem
Illustrations © 2004 by Kevin Ingram

Published by Fleming H. Revell
a division of Baker Book House Company
P.O. Box 6287, Grand Rapids, MI 49516-6287
www.bakerbooks.com

Printed in the United States of America

Library of Congress Cataloging-in-Publication Data
Tatem, Mary.
    Beautiful threads : pieces of encouragement for quilters / Mary
Tatem.
        p.   cm.
    ISBN 0-8007-5932-X (pbk.)
    1. Women—Religious life. 2. Quilting—Religious aspects—Christi-
anity. I. Title.
BV4527.T37 2004
242′.643—dc22   2003022914

To my children—
Joe, Becky, Andy, and Matthew—
who form beautiful threads in the fabric of the future
and provide my life with encouragement and joy.

Contents

· Contents ·

Between the Stitches

In the making of a quilt, how distracted I can be, basting stitches, pinning together pieces, tying up all the loose, colorful threads. It's enough detail work to make anyone lose sight of the beautiful result.

Isn't that just like life?

The daily grind, chores, events, personalities, and demands we face any given day or season can make us lose sight of God's beautiful design.

Yet we are his workmanship, the Scriptures tell us (Eph. 2:10). God created us with more enthusiasm than the most excited quilter ever experienced when piecing just the right scraps into a stunning new coverlet. With infinite tenderness, God is busy at work, taking what's frayed here or worn there and creating something new, beautiful, and purposeful. Beyond all the details in our process of living, this Craftsman has his eye on a beautiful design—a perfect pattern and plan for you, me, and every one of his creatures—if only we have the eyes to see.

Think of this book, then, as one offering you a step back from the piecework of your life—as something to wrap up in when you need an encouraging break or bright perspective. This collection, based on true stories, centered on a dozen of the most popular patterns in America, will remind you that God weaves beautiful threads around us every day—and always relentlessly, tirelessly. He is, after all, a most focused father and friend.

While you're sure to recognize the designs featured here, the names might sometimes surprise you. The same quilt pattern can be called different names in various regions of the world and eras of history. This, too, relates a spiritual truth. The names of the roles God calls us to perform are not as important as the beauty of the design he's creating in each life; he appreciates the seed of his design in each of us, even when we're unable to recognize it.

It's a good reminder as you read these reflections for quilting and for your spiritual life: The work of God in us is not yet finished.

Grandmother's Flower Garden

Sometimes called Mosaic, the Grandmother's Flower Garden pattern became a favorite in magazines, which published its directions as early as 1835. The pattern gets its name from blending lighter-shaded pieces with progressively deeper-colored ones until—*voila!*—a flower bed seems to appear in full bloom. Since a finished quilt can consist of thousands of hexagons, and some seamstresses cut their pieces as tiny as five-eighths of an inch, the pattern truly becomes a showpiece.

It's the same way with our lives, isn't it? The light and dark colors of our life experiences blend subtly but artfully in the hands of the one with the master pattern, until finally they burst into spectacular blooms. In this section, a German schoolboy, a damaged heirloom, a Valentine's Day surprise, and a box of buttons form stories that reveal the varied hues we find weaving through all of our lives—and the beauty that can arise, with God's skillful guidance, from each one.

Nimble Fingers

"I don't want to take knitting and sewing." Otto stood beside his teacher's desk, clenched fists on his hips.

"That doesn't matter, Otto. The school system requires all ten-year-olds to learn knitting and sewing." Mrs. Wagner's eyes twinkled at the same time she frowned at Otto.

"But why? Boys don't need to sew and knit. Girls do that. Please, Mrs. Wagner, none of us boys wants to sew."

"Our German government has made these skills a requirement for years and years."

"But this is 1960. Now boys run big machines." Otto bent over the desk.

"When you grow up, you may need to sew on your buttons."

"I'll get married, and my Frau will do that."

"I thought you wanted to be a doctor," Mrs. Wagner said, patting his fist. "Did you know that surgeons knit, quilt, and embroider to improve their fine-muscle coordination, which makes them more skilled in surgery?"

"Maybe I won't be a doctor after all," Otto responded with a pout. "Maybe I'll move to America. I'll bet American boys don't sew in school."

"In Germany, we want our boys to be well rounded with well-developed fine-muscle skills."

"I don't want to be well rounded." Otto patted his tummy.

"Regardless, this year we learn knitting and sewing. You may as well decide to enjoy it."

Otto wasn't mollified. On his way home from school, he detoured his bicycle to his family doctor's office.

"I quilt to unwind from the tensions of my job and to keep my fingers nimble for surgery," Dr. Bogart confirmed. "Do you want to see my work?"

Dr. Bogart led Otto back to his office. This wasn't the room Otto saw when he went to Dr. Bogart for stitches in his knees or pills for his sore throat. Hanging on the wall was a large quilt made of thousands of hexagons arranged in colorful rings, ranging from light to dark blues.

"You didn't make that, did you?" Otto couldn't contain his surprise.

"I did, and I'm very proud of it. The pattern is called Grandmother's Flower Garden, and it requires precision to get those six sides to match up properly with all the other hexagons." Dr. Bogart traced the outline of one flower with his finger. "Don't be fooled, young man. Men, with their geometric instincts, do a superior job of piecing the kind of quilt patterns that require careful measuring, cutting, and matching."

"It looks nice," Otto admitted.

"Sure does, but when I first started to learn, I couldn't have done such a large project. I grew more skilled as I practiced. It's the same with anything in life, especially doctoring. If you want to do something well, you start with small steps, practice, and apply yourself until you become more proficient. Our German schools do a good job of training young people. Be thankful for your school years."

"I want to be a doctor."

"Then learn every one of your school subjects well," Dr. Bogart said and shook Otto's hand. "Sewing among them!"

The Master Pattern

I have hidden your word in my heart
that I might not sin against you.

Psalm 119:11

Whether we are young or old, learning equips us with skills that will help us live productive lives. The most fruitful study for a satisfying life is the Bible. By reading and meditating on God's Word, we gain understanding of how God wants us to live. He warns us about courses of action that will bring us only grief. Best of all, we grow in our understanding of who God is and how much he cares for us. Knowledge of God multiplies the joy in our lives.

God, help me make daily Bible study a firm habit, so my love for you might blossom like a flower garden.

Frayed Edges

Erin paused in her reading to look up at her husband's picture on the mantel. She frowned at her smiling man. He never fawned over her the way a romance novel hero would. *Bill is so unromantic compared to this guy,* she thought.

He was downright clumsy when it came to compliments, not to mention more intimate things. Feeling her level of dissatisfaction with her spouse climb, Erin buried herself back in her book. Bill's romantic stock continued to fall as she read.

Erin jerked her head as the doorbell's harsh buzz abruptly broke into her fantasy. She slammed her book shut and uncurled from her comfortable reading position, hastily stuffing the book under the couch.

"Coming, coming." Irritation at the interruption of her story edged Erin's voice. Before starting toward the door, she checked to make sure the plaid sofa skirt fell back down to conceal her book. She peeked in the mirror hanging beside the front entrance. Relieved she didn't look as flushed as her cheeks felt, she tucked a lock of hair behind her ear and opened the door.

A small, neatly dressed woman stood on the step. "Hi, I'm Lisa, from the church down the street." She waved toward a white church steeple visible from the door. "We were so glad to have you worship with us Sunday. I'm on the visiting committee and came to welcome you to our congregation." She offered some brochures to Erin.

"Come in." Erin took the brochures and hoped Lisa didn't detect her slight hesitation before she opened the door wide.

Lisa followed Erin into her apartment, stopping to admire her wedding portrait hanging in the entryway.

When Lisa exclaimed about how attractive the living room looked, Erin forgot her annoyance at having to stop reading in the middle of a steamy love scene in her book. Lisa made a quick tour of the room, admiring Erin's decorative touches.

"Did you quilt this?" Lisa stood in front of a small wall hanging.

"Yes, but I'm just learning. I decided to try my hand at quilting when I inherited my Grandmother's Flower Garden quilt. It's one of my most treasured possessions. All the lavender printed fabrics blend together to make it really look like a flower garden full of blooms."

"It sounds lovely. May I see it?"

"Sure. I've had it stashed away among the things we left in storage while we were stationed overseas." Erin led the way into her dining area and lifted the flaps of a cardboard box. "Even with the colors muted by age, I think it's gorgeous," she said, picking it up.

Both women gasped. A small, gray mouse escaped from the folds of the quilt and darted from the dining room into the living room and under the sofa. Startled, Erin chased after it and dropped the quilt onto the couch. Lisa followed. She got down on her hands and knees, picked up the sofa skirt, and peered under for the intruder.

"I don't see any signs of the mouse. But this book must have gotten kicked under here." Sitting back on her heels, Lisa handed it to Erin.

Feeling a hot flush creep across her face, Erin tried to conceal her embarrassment with a nonchalant look. Glad for the brown paper concealing its torrid cover picture and suggestive title, she tossed it into her magazine rack. To deflect Lisa's attention, Erin spread out her quilt.

"No! No!" Erin stared in horror at holes perfectly spaced wherever the quilt had been folded. "It's ruined. That awful mouse has destroyed my grandmother's quilt." She wailed in spite of having company.

"What a shame." Lisa leaned over to examine the damage. "You know, I have a friend who mends heirloom quilts. If you'd like, I could ask her to look at yours and see if she can fix it. It probably won't look quite the same, but you could fold it just right and still enjoy its beauty. Who knows? It might turn out better than we think. She says rodents and insects are a common cause of damage."

After a nice visit, in which Lisa talked with excitement about how God was blessing the lives of the people in her congregation, she left, promising to let Erin know what her quilt-repairing friend said.

Erin sank down on the sofa and took a deep breath. The smell of her Grandmother's Flower Garden quilt triggered happy memories. She sat for a long time, cuddling the quilt in her arms. She thought about how dissatisfied she sometimes felt with her marriage, as if it had little holes in it like the quilt. What was eating at the delight she'd once felt for her husband?

Spotting the erotic book angled in the rack, she stood, snatched it up, and carried it into the kitchen, where she threw it into the garbage can.

"These trashy books are making me feel as if there are holes in my marriage as certainly as that nasty mouse chewed holes in my quilt," she proclaimed to the pot of African violets on her kitchen counter. "These books are unrealistic. No wonder I'm feeling discontented with my husband." Erin turned away and searched in her cabinet for a mousetrap. "And it's the trash for you, too, chomping rodent."

The Master Pattern

Catch for us the foxes,
the little foxes
that ruin the vineyards,
our vineyards that are in bloom.

Song of Songs 2:15

We can easily ignore or excuse small sins, but so-called little transgressions can prevent our lives from blooming with the beauty we desire. While the damage of glaring sin is obvious, allowing worldly ideas to creep into our thinking will also damage the good fruit we want to grow in our lives. Let us ask God to make us aware when we allow a compromise, anything big or small, that conflicts with the purity God wants for us. It's a simple matter to seek forgiveness. And God will help us chase the little foxes out of our lives, so that our vineyard is fruitful.

God, I'm sorry that I so often fail to live up to the standards of Scripture. Thank you for showing me areas of my life I can change in order to find greater joy. Thank you for loving me just as I am. Please continue to mature me.

A Quilted Reminder

Jackie leaned over Chris's quilt, curling her upper lip in distaste. "Yuck! You're putting pieces of pink, red, and orange next to each other. Don't you think they clash?"

"I'm having enough trouble getting these little pieces to match up right. Don't tell me I'm doing the colors wrong, too." Chris frowned as she sat with the other women gathered around a long table for a quilting class.

"Your quilt is pretty, Chris," Laura reassured her. "Pinks, reds, and oranges go together in real flower gardens. Since you're making a Grandmother's Flower Garden quilt, I think they blend just fine."

"We've been working on the projects for so long, I'd think you'd have your Flower Garden quilt further along," grumbled Jackie as she continued to find fault.

Chris swallowed a retort about the critical atmosphere freezing the flowers in her quilt garden. She struggled for more patience with the querulous Jackie and reached into her purse. Wondering if the grumpy woman had forgotten breakfast and was the victim of a blood-sugar crash, she pulled out a bag of M&M's. "Have some Valentine candy," she said, emptying the bag into a bowl in the center of the table.

"Look, even M&M's put red and pink together for Valentine's," Laura said, taking a handful.

"But they used white, not orange, with them," Jackie countered. "Anyway, aren't we too old to celebrate Valentine's Day?"

"Speak for yourself. My husband and I went out for dinner, and he gave me a beautiful tennis bracelet." Laura held her arm out for the other women to admire the gleaming jewelry.

As others chimed in with what they did for Valentine's Day, Jackie frowned. "Well, I think giving gifts for Valentine's Day is kids' stuff."

Chris ignored her. "Speaking of gifts, every year I give myself the most important Valentine gift," she said, looking around the table.

"What's that?" Jackie sniffed.

"Well, it's a gift each one of you should give yourself every February." Chris pointed her needle at the others for emphasis.

"I don't need any more candy or sweets," Laura said, patting her hips with a wry laugh.

"Everyone needs this gift, and you give it to yourself because you love yourself."

"What's the point of a gift if you have to buy it for yourself?" Jackie said. "If you ask me, some people love themselves a little too much."

"Ah, but Jesus cared for you enough to buy you eternal life with the price of his blood. If he loves us so much, and God was pleased when he made us, it's okay to love ourselves. You're worth the best gift: life. Want to know what I buy myself every Valentine's Day?"

The needles grew still around the table, and the women looked toward Chris.

"Every February, I have a mammogram to check for any abnormalities or lumps. I do it in February, because Valentine's Day helps me remember I owe it to God to take care of the body he loved enough to die for."

The women murmured assent.

"This year, I'm especially glad I've made this an annual routine, because the mammogram showed a suspicious place, and a biopsy confirmed it was cancer."

A chorus of shocked reactions surrounded her.

"No, Chris!"

"That's not something to be glad about!"

"That's awful. Why didn't you tell us sooner?"

"Cancer—now that's a gift I can do without," Jackie said.

"No, really. I'm so glad I've been faithful to have the test. This is how the doctor discovered this spot, even though it's so small, it's almost microscopic." Chris laid her hand over her heart. "The doctor feels sure that with some radiation, I'll be fine. The mammogram meant I found out in time to save my life. I call that a top-notch gift."

As the weeks of medical treatment progressed, Chris sometimes thought plying a needle to her quilt felt as strenuous as hoeing a row in the garden. Her dream of finishing the quilt that year faded, and she put her half-completed project away to work on during another season.

Some months later, after she finally completed her Grandmother's Flower Garden quilt, she used its prominent display in her living room to remind her guests that a Valentine present of a mammogram is a wonderful gift of love.

The Master Pattern

We love because he first loved us.

1 John 4:19

When we realize that God loved us with an intensity that caused him to send his only Son, Jesus, to die on the cross, in order that we might spend eternity with him, we find the freedom to love ourselves. In gratitude for the love of God, we should take good care of the bodies he created for us. Because he loved us when we were unworthy and unlovable, we should love him. Out of that love grows love for others, even when they are cantankerous like Jackie. We find that our dispositions improve when we are secure in God's love.

Lord, whenever I'm around disagreeable people, help me remember that you love all your creations. Make your love for me so real that it molds my approach to life. Show me ways to take good care of this wonderful body you created for me.

26

Buttoned into Our Memory

"Meow."

Melanie abruptly returned from her daydream when her cat bumped against her hand, causing her to drop a handful of buttons into her lap. "Mittens, who let you in?"

"I did." Julie, Melanie's next-door neighbor, appeared in the doorway of her family room. "I could see you through the window, but you didn't seem to hear my knock."

"Sorry, I didn't hear you. I was sorting through these boxes of Kevin's college things. We brought them home after the funeral."

"Oh, am I interrupting a painful chore? I can come back later."

"It's all right. Actually, these buttons bring back pleasant memories." Melanie picked up a handful and let them sift through her fingers back into her lap. "Kevin thought I was crazy, supposing he would need buttons to replace the ones he might lose off his shirts. Boy, he sure teased me when I put this box of buttons in with his things to take to college. He howled with laughter." In spite of her red-rimmed eyes, Melanie smiled.

"He said he'd bring his shirts home for me to fix. I told him that learning to wield a needle to reattach buttons was as important a part of his education as any logarithm problem he'd encounter."

Melanie suddenly stood up, scattering buttons and a startled cat. She began to pace. "He didn't get to sew buttons or do logarithm problems. Or graduate, or get married, or finish growing up."

She sighed and sank onto her knees, then began to pick up the buttons and return them to their box. Julie knelt down to help her.

Melanie sat and rubbed one of the buttons between her fingers. "Makes me feel close to him, somehow. I know it seems ridiculous, but the sight of these buttons is comforting. The memory of joking about them with Kevin is a good one."

Julie sat back on her heels. "That gives me an idea. Have you given any more thought about going to the quilting class with me? Since the class is to make a Grandmother's Flower Garden quilt, you could sew a button on the centerpiece of each flower. You would have good memories at your fingertips wherever you put the quilt."

Melanie picked up some more buttons. "I'd have enough buttons, that's for sure. Look at all of them! Kevin joked that I must've thought he was going to lose a couple a day. I think the buttons were my way of trying to make sure he was well equipped for his new life. You wonder if you have prepared your child enough when you send him off." Her voice broke. "I didn't. Prepare him enough, that is.

Didn't I remember to teach him not to ride with someone who was drunk?"

"You did teach him, Melanie," Julie said, reaching over the buttons to gather her friend in her arms. "You did your very best to prepare him for life. Concentrate on thinking about the happy times."

"Okay." Melanie pulled a tissue out of a box on an end table and blew her nose. "I'll make the quilt and keep it on my sofa, and then I'll make another for his brother. In fact, I'll sew one of Kevin's buttons onto everything I make for gifts from now on. The whole family can remember him."

Melanie's watery smile brought Mittens to her lap with a purr. "With this many, I can make something for every niece and nephew with at least one or two buttons on it, so they'll go on remembering Kevin. And watching out for drunk drivers."

The Master Pattern

And when he had given thanks, he broke [the bread] and said, "This is my body, which is for you; do this in remembrance of me." In the same way, after supper he took the cup, saying, "This cup is the new covenant in my blood; do this, whenever you drink it, in remembrance of me."

1 Corinthians 11:24–25

Memory operates in curious ways. The most trivial objects, such as the buttons for Melanie, can trigger a past memory. Even a smell can remind us of a loved one who passed away long ago. As time goes on, though, our memories may grow faint. God must have realized our human frailty when he initiated communion.

When we take communion, it stirs our memories and fills us once again with gratitude for Jesus' enormous sacrifice. We remember the high price he paid so we might have eternal life, and we are motivated to spread the message of Jesus to those who do not know him.

God, help me to remember your great sacrifice for me and to tell others of your provision of eternal life.

Dresden Plate

Named for the German city of Dresden's famous china,
this pattern features delicate floral fabric that's pieced into
circles resembling porcelain plates. The most common plate
is made of wedges that are either scalloped or pointed
at the outer rim. Usually Dresden Plate quilt borders are
scalloped, with the edges following the rounded lines of
the edges of the plates. By the 1930s, quilters refined the
Dresden Plate design by cutting wedges from a variety of

dry-goods sacks—mostly pastel shades—and piecing them in a round.

As the following stories show, even chicken-feed sacks can provide lovely fabric for the committed quilter, and quilting can be more than a delightful hobby. It might also build a road out of poverty, form a loving memorial to a departed friend, and make fingers agile for other delicate work. The beautiful threads of God's commitment to our well-being form the foundation for every positive outcome.

Floral Fabric and Chicken Feed

"Be careful!" Marie's hand darted over the dishpan, rescuing her Blue Willow china plate just as it slipped from Jenny's sudsy fingers.

"I'm sorry, Mommy." The six-year-old moved over to give her mother room by the basin.

"I know." Marie dunked the dish into the rinse-water pan. "I guess I should wash the Blue Willow plates myself, since I always feel so bad when another one breaks." She dried the dish and stood it beside four other plates on the wooden plate rack decorating the wall. "My mother wanted me to treasure these dishes as much as she did."

"If they all break, you still have the pretty plates you're making on your quilt," Jenny said, pointing to the partially finished quilt spread on a chair close to the window.

Marie laughed. "We can't eat off of them, even if the pattern is called Dresden Plate! And those 'plates' weren't handed down to me from my grandmother." She grew wistful. "But at least a fabric plate on a quilt won't break, if your father gets a notion to move us farther west again."

"I'd like to move closer to a city, so we could have running water," Sarah said with a sigh as she picked up the galvanized dishpan. As the bigger sister, she carried the pan to the front step and poured the water on the rosebush growing outside.

"It would cost us more to live in a city," Marie reminded her. She took up the quilt she was working on and noted, "I need some more fabric to complete this design."

"You could make a prettier quilt if we lived in the city," Sarah said, reemphasizing her preference.

"Why would that be?"

"You could buy store cloth instead of using old chicken-feed sacks for the design." Sarah waved a hand of disdain toward the quilt.

"And pay more for it," Marie said, rummaging through her basket of fabric scraps. "I'm grateful the companies make chicken-feed sacks out of such pretty material. I rather like the muted look of the colors."

"Thanks, chickens!" Jenny tried to cackle.

"Why are we grateful to the chickens?" Marshall stopped in the doorway to dust barnyard straw off his overalls, then stepped in and held out his arms to his two daughters. "Besides thanking chickens for our breakfast eggs and delicious Sunday dinners, that is."

"We like the chicken-feed sacks." Jenny giggled when her father tickled her tummy.

"We do, and I need another bag so I can finish this Dresden Plate quilt," Marie said, holding out a swatch of cloth to her husband. "The chicken feed looks low in the bag,

Marshall. When you go to buy more, please search through the bags to find one that matches this blue floral pattern." She tucked the scrap into his hand.

"Do you realize how silly I would look to the men at the store, insisting on a certain chicken-feed bag?"

"Thrifty is silly?" Marie raised her eyebrows.

"Anything for my frugal sweetheart." Marshall slipped the material into his pocket, reached past his clinging girls, and planted a tender kiss on his wife's forehead. "Not every man is blessed with a woman who doesn't scorn commonplace items but uses them wisely."

The Master Pattern

His master replied, "Well done, good and faithful servant! You have been faithful with a few things; I will put you in charge of many things. Come and share your master's happiness!"

Matthew 25:21

A wise person takes time to feel grateful for the little delights in life. One secret of contentment is not to overlook small, everyday blessings. When we give thanks for the ordinary objects and occurrences in our lives, we open our hearts to larger portions of joy: We feel an even greater appreciation for the larger, less-frequent pleasures when they come.

Lord, help me not to overlook small reasons for thanksgiving. Help me to celebrate even the seemingly mundane gifts of each day.

Stitching a Way Out

Star bent forward against the wind. Her mittened hand scraped a layer of ice off the scarf that protected her nose and mouth against the snow and bitter cold. Beside her, Gentle Fawn hung on to her arm. Both girls walked slowly. The driving snow made the landmarks hard to see on the route from their Indian village to the closest Nevada town.

"Maybe we should turn back," Gentle Fawn said, tugging at Star's arm. She wished her fear of getting lost would vanish as easily as her voice did on the wind.

When Star didn't hear her, Gentle Fawn planted her feet and held Star back with both hands. Putting her mouth close to Star's ear, she shouted over the wind, "We should have stayed home today. We'll get lost in this storm."

"No, we won't. Don't look at the white nothingness. Look down. We can see the road. Today, the wind is our friend. The road doesn't have anything to stop the snow, so the wind keeps sweeping it clear. As long as we can see the road, we can follow it into town."

"Why are we stopping?" yelled one of the other four girls from the reservation.

"It's too cold to stop," another said.

"It's only one more mile to the quilt cooperative. Let's go."

The four moved on, and Star ran to catch up, pulling Gentle Fawn behind her.

When the girls finally reached the cooperative, Mrs. Grover and her assistant, Beth, pulled the girls inside, unwrapped their frozen mufflers, and led them to a large kerosene heater in the middle of the plain, wood-framed room.

"I'm surprised you came today," Mrs. Grover said, pulling a quilting frame closer to the warm stove.

"We had to come," Star said. "The money we earn working for your quilt cooperative buys food for my little brothers at home."

"I saved the Dresden Plate quilt for you girls to work on if you made it in today." Mrs. Grover indicated the pretty top already on the frame and basted to batting and backing. "These beautiful circles of bright wedges deserve my best quilters. Such a fine quilt will earn a good sum."

"Our fingers are so numb." Star held her hands over the stove and squeezed them open and shut to get some circulation back in them.

Mrs. Grover took Star's hand and began to rub her fingers gently. "Are you starting to get some feeling back yet? It wouldn't do to stick your fingers and bleed on the fabric."

"This will help," Beth said, carrying in a tray with steaming cups of hot chocolate for the girls.

As the hot drink warmed their insides and the heater warmed them on the outside, the girls began to relax. "See," Star whispered to Gentle Fawn. "I told you not to look at the nothingness of the snow. I knew that if God made a road with the quilt cooperative to help our families, he could make a road to follow in the storm."

The Master Pattern

And my God will meet all your needs according to his glorious riches in Christ Jesus.

Philippians 4:19

Whether our concern is relief from poverty, comfort in times of grief, or aid in illness, God's resources are available to meet our needs. When we take our serious or small problems to God, his supply is unlimited. What's more, he finds delight in taking care of us. And he often gives us the privilege of working for, or in some way contributing to, our provision.

Lord, I bring my needs to you, trusting in your riches for what I lack.

38

Quilt-Square Memorial

Martha looped one arm through Anna's and handed her a tissue as they walked from the cemetery to the church.

"I guess funerals do serve a purpose," Anna said, wiping her eyes. "The ceremony helped me accept the reality that Jane died. Ever since her daughter called Monday with the news, I've felt like it was a bad dream. I kept thinking I'd wake up, and we'd go to the quilting guild together, just like always." A shudder shook Anna's shoulders. "But we won't."

Martha dabbed at her own eyes. "I'm surprised how well Susan is holding up. There never was a closer mother-daughter relationship."

"My goodness! Maybe this helped." Anna stopped in the doorway of the church's fellowship hall, where Jane's family was receiving friends. "It looks as if Susan has spent the days between Jane's death and the funeral creating a memorial for her mother."

"What a fitting tribute to our creative friend," Martha said, gesturing toward the colorful quilts, hung one beside another and covering two entire walls. "I didn't realize how many quilts she'd made."

"What beautiful work she did! I'm going to miss sitting in her living room, stitching our projects together. She always had a suggestion for piecing, or cutting and stitching, that saved time or made the quilt look better."

Anna started at the right, and together the two women joined the many others who made a tour of their friend's productive hobby. When the friends reached Susan, Martha said, "These quilts make me sad and glad at the same time. Jane was a cheerful person. It's like some sunshine has been taken out of my life. We're going to miss your mother."

"What a nice thing to say, and how true! I'm going to put that in my memory bank for the blue days when I want her back. She did leave a lot of cheer and laughter behind, didn't she?"

Anna took Susan's hand. "I'll never see a quilt but that I'll think of your mother."

At the next quilt guild meeting, the women were unusually quiet. Martha grumbled, "Can't someone think of something to say?" Everyone felt Jane's absence.

When Susan swept into the room with a basket on her arm, the atmosphere changed in less time than it took to cut out a calico square. "Mother talked about how she loved each of you and your times quilting together," she told the group. "I think she would like it if I gave each of you one of the Dresden Plate squares she made. She had finished the squares but hadn't sewn them together into a quilt top."

Each lady took home a fitting memorial to her fellow quilter, Jane. Martha made a little pillow from the square to put on her living-room sofa, and Anna sewed a wall hanging. All the ladies were grateful to own something their friend had created with her own hands.

The Master Pattern

Tell them that the flow of the Jordan was cut off before the ark of the covenant of the LORD. When it crossed the Jordan, the waters of the Jordan were cut off. These stones are to be a memorial to the people of Israel forever.

Joshua 4:7

In the Old Testament, people often built memorials of stone to mark important events. When the Israelites crossed the flooded Jordan into Canaan, God stopped the flow of upstream water, and the nation crossed over safely. Joshua instructed one man from each of the twelve tribes to take a stone from the middle of the riverbed as he crossed. He was to carry it to the other side, where they made a memorial from the stones. It served as a sign of God's faithfulness in providing them with a miraculous crossing.

Finding small ways to honor the memory of a loved one brings comfort and shows appreciation to God for the life he created. We give glory to God when we remember important events in our lives and thank him for them.

God, make my words and actions magnify you in the events you daily orchestrate in my life. Help me carry happy memories to comfort those who have lost loved ones.

41

A Stitch in Time . . .

"May I help you?" George took the jeweler's monocle from his eye and looked at the girl clutching her purse in front of the ring counter. To his surprise, his concentration on his engraving had been so intense, he'd missed the ring of the bell when the girl had opened the store's door.

"I hope so, but it does seem like an awfully lot to ask of you," Cora answered, looking down at the floor.

"Ask away. We aim to please at George and Sons Jewelry." George slid down from the tall stool, putting his tool with the others spread out on a workbench. "Challenges contribute to our reputation as Bowling Green's finest. Do you see a ring you like?" George pointed into the display case. "Is there an engagement coming up?"

"Oh, no, I already have the ring. It's the engraving I need." Cora hurried on breathlessly, "It's so small a space, and it already has initials and dates engraved on it, so there isn't much room. But Harry thinks it's ever so important to use his mother's ring. He thinks it would mean good luck for our marriage and . . ." Cora's voice trailed off. Her eyes met George's. At the twinkle she found there, she lowered her eyes again as if embarrassed.

"Let's see this remarkable ring with the power to make or break a marriage."

Cora was already digging in her purse. "Here. Harry's mother died five years ago, and he wants to use her ring to make her a part of the wedding. But the band is very small. Do you think it's possible to engrave our initials and wedding date beside Harry's parents' engraving?" Cora handed the thin gold band to George.

"If anyone in Kentucky can do it, I can. You've come to the right place." George flexed his fingers. "I have a secret way to keep my fingers nimble, and I'm up to the challenge." He turned the ring around and around in his hand. "What are your initials, and what is the wedding date?"

"Well, we'll be married this year, 1935. I wanted to have the wedding on Friday, the thirteenth, four months from today, but Harry thought that date would bring bad luck. So we'll be married on the fourteenth instead."

George gave her a piercing stare. "Little lady, are you sure you want to marry a man who hangs on to his dead mother and is steeped in superstition?" When he saw her face fall, he said, "Oh, I beg your pardon. I shouldn't have said anything."

Cora looked down. "You aren't the first to say that. My Bible study group keeps telling me Christians don't need superstitions. They warn me to make sure Harry is a Christian."

She tried to turn the direction of the conversation. "Why do you think your fingers can do more delicate work than other jewelers' can?"

43

"I'll show you my secret of conquering engraving challenges if you'll challenge this young man of yours about his belief in God."

George pulled a basket from under his counter and spread out a dozen quilt squares with Dresden Plates neatly appliquéd in place. "I keep my fingers limber by quilting. The smaller I make my stitches, the better I train my fingers and make them agile for engraving. I make lots of quilts to give me good control over my hands. It's just like when you study the Bible with your study group, you train your mind to make decisions God's way."

George held the ring in the palm of his hand. "Ready for me to use my skills on Harry's mother's ring?"

Cora took the ring back. "I'll talk to Harry. I don't even know if he reads his Bible. Thanks—I'll think about what you said."

The Master Pattern

Have nothing to do with godless myths and old wives' tales; rather, train yourself to be godly. For physical training is of some value, but godliness has value for all things, holding promise for both the present life and the life to come.

1 Timothy 4:7–8

Disciplined training benefits our bodies and our minds. The Bible tells us our bodies are the temples of the Holy Spirit, so we honor God when we keep ourselves fit. Even more important to our well-being is the exercising of our spiritual muscles. When we focus intently on discovering the mind of God and are determined to follow his will, we will find that our lives carry greater value to the world around us and bring us more joy.

Lord, I want to be spiritually fit. Help me to study faithfully and follow your ways.

Sunbonnet Sue

In the 1880s, Sunbonnet Sue began as an embroidery pattern for the outline of a girl. Since a wide-brimmed hat hid her face, the tedious embroidery of facial features was unnecessary. Quilters adapted this design by cutting dresses and hats from pretty fabrics, then appliquéing them to a different background cloth. In 1902, an illustrator gave Sunbonnet Sue a large, billowing skirt for appliqué. The designer believed the position of the body and the drape of the skirt could convey emotion even without showing the figure's face.

In these stories, emotion often overwhelms the quilter or the quilt owner, sometimes with positive results, sometimes not. Blemished fabric, an unexpected donation, faulty measurements, and a hurricane's fury inspire feelings of panic, bewilderment, joy, and satisfaction. God's remedies include faith and forgiveness, cooperation and compassion, and they reveal the beautiful threads we can grasp in every circumstance.

Spotted Bonnets

"Wouldn't that wall look great decorated with a quilt?" Ellie asked, pointing to the area behind the podium where the spring festival speaker would stand.

"I second that idea. With our pioneer theme and a quilting speaker, it's the perfect backdrop. Everybody agree?" Marge saw the nods around the table.

"Anybody own a quilt we could use?" Ellie asked.

No one raised her hand, and Marge's shoulders sagged. "Maybe our perfect idea won't work."

"Maybe it will. I almost forgot that I have my grandmother's Sunbonnet Sue quilt. It's been stored for years and years in a cedar chest at home," Joy said. "I'll bring it."

After supper, when Joy dug through her cedar chest and pulled out her grandmother's quilt, her shoulders sagged with more discouragement than Marge's had. The heirloom was speckled with brown spots. At her horrified cry, her family came running.

"I can't hang a ruined quilt behind the club's speaker!"

49

"Don't give up yet," her husband, Les, encouraged. "We've weeks yet to try to get the spots out."

Joy tried and tried. A friend suggested lemon juice. A book mentioned Murphy's Oil soap. Alcohol didn't help, and Joy was afraid bleach would be too harsh on such old fabric. Eyeglass cleaner faded the stains a little. After using dishwasher detergent with some small benefit, Joy gave up. Disappointed, she took the very clean but still blemished quilt to her committee.

"The Sunbonnet Girls are still pretty. I like the different colors and designs for each of the girl's dresses," Ellie said.

"It looks old, that's for sure. But isn't that appropriate for a pioneer theme? After all, covered-wagon days were a long time ago." Marge held the quilt up and backed away from the others. "From a distance, don't you notice its attractive design more than the spots? I say, let's use it. It's for background atmosphere. The speaker will be the center of attention."

"Next time, don't store a quilt against bare wood," noted Ellie as she rubbed her hand over a faint brown spot.

Joy nodded and smiled, relieved that her offering was acceptable, in spite of her error of storing her treasured comforter in a wooden chest. Her smile broadened when she thought how God accepted her in spite of her mistakes.

The Master Pattern

Christ loved the church and gave himself up for her to make her holy, cleansing her by the washing with water through the word, and to present her to himself as a radiant church, without stain or wrinkle or any other blemish, but holy and blameless.

Ephesians 5:25–27

Joy's best efforts could not remove the blotches on her quilt. It's the same with the stain sin leaves on our souls. No amount of effort or discipline eliminates the scar of sin.

The difficulty of life and the frailty of our humanity make it impossible to stand before God without stain or wrinkle. Instead of despairing over this certainty, Christians find great gladness because they understand that Jesus shed his blood to cover their sin. Unlike the various cleaning substances Joy used on her quilt, the blood of Jesus completely removes the blot of our sins and makes us clean in the eyes of God.

Jesus, thank you for dying on the cross for my sin. Help me to repent quickly when I fail to live up to the standards of the Word of God.

Same Stitches, Different Views

"Would next weekend work for my visit?" The background noise of Liz's flipping pages of her daily planner mingled with her voice.

"Sure. The guest room is always ready for you. We haven't seen you since Grandma Lawrence's funeral," Holly said as she wrote Liz's name on the calendar square for the weekend.

"Sorry I left you with all the cleaning and disposing of Grandma's things." Liz didn't sound as if she really regretted missing those chores. "Guess I stay too busy with church commitments."

"Anything special you want to do while you're here?" Holly held her pen poised over her calendar.

"I think the main thing is to go through the boxes of Grandma's things you've been sorting. Since I'm driving, I can bring home some keepsakes. I especially want to see her snapshots and her quilt."

Holly dropped her pen. "I've taken some things to the Salvation Army," she said slowly, "but there is still plenty of stuff left in boxes here." *And you're not going to applaud my solution for what to do about one quilt for three granddaughters,* she thought. "Looking forward to seeing you."

But she wasn't. She wished she had the nerve to tell Liz about the quilt on the phone, but her courage failed her. Instead, she said, "I'll tell Rachel you're coming. She'll want to be here if we divide up the snapshots."

After hanging up the phone, Holly headed straight for her car and drove to nearby Western Branch University, the alma mater for three generations of Lawrence women. She parked at the university library and museum. As soon as she stepped inside the library, she clapped her hands and grinned.

"Looks great, doesn't it?" The museum docent smiled at Holly.

"I never imagined how great," Holly said, beaming as she looked up at Grandma's Sunbonnet Sue quilt.

But when Holly took Liz and Rachel to see where Grandma's quilt now resided, its looking great wasn't enough to mollify the two siblings.

"I still think the university is the perfect place to display it," Holly said to defend herself when her sisters complained. "Each Sunbonnet Sue wears a dress made from material given to Grandma by a relative of a fallen Vietnam War hero. All the little flags the girls carry display the names of war heroes who attended our alma mater."

She hurried on, trying to make Liz and Rachel see how appropriate the gift of the quilt was to the college: "The docent says a steady stream of townsfolk are coming to look at it. They read the names of the servicepeople embroidered on the girls' flags and talk about their memories of them when they were on campus." Holly gestured toward others standing close to the quilt.

"People are looking all right," Liz said, staring at an unkempt woman standing near the quilt. "What were you thinking, putting Grandma's quilt where weird people will look at it?"

Holly sank down on a bench. "I thought about how important this college was to Grandma. Don't you think she'd like knowing her work was bringing enjoyment to lots of people?"

The Master Pattern

He said to them, "Go into all the world and preach the good news to all creation."

Mark 16:15

Holly wasn't successful in convincing her sisters to think about the pleasure her grandmother's quilt could bring to people beyond the immediate family. All the two sisters thought of was how ill-groomed the people in the museum were and how differently they dressed themselves. Christians need to remember that the gospel of Jesus Christ, which brings us joy and peace, is something God tells us not to relegate inside our churches. The gospel is for all people, even those who seem "different." God commands us to take the Good News of Jesus beyond our familiar walls and community.

God, give me a deeper understanding of the need all people have of Christ, regardless of how unusual or intimidating they seem to me. Help me to use my resources to take the gospel to others.

Work's Reward

"Finished." Jim put his hammer down and brushed hair back from his forehead, viewing the quilt display racks with satisfaction.

"Wishful thinking," Judy said and patted his shoulder. "You're not finished until you assemble them in the community room the day before the quilt festival."

"I hope that after I built all these racks, your quilt wins first prize."

"What a system that would be! The quilt maker whose husband did the most work wins. I'd win every time." Judy grinned at her husband.

"Yeah, if my work were what it took for my sweetheart to come home with the ribbons, I'd be selling the raffle tickets and pounding the pavement for advertisers, too." Jim winked. "If I were the judge, you'd win. You make beautiful quilts."

"Thanks for building all these racks."

"You're worth it." Jim dropped a kiss on her head.

The next evening, he wasn't so sure anything was worth it. After dinner, he had driven to the community room to set up the racks, and Judy had accompanied him to help arrange the displays.

"You told me ten-foot-tall racks," Jim said, scratching his head. "I know that's what you told me."

"Yeah, so what's the problem?" Judy said.

"Judy, the ceilings are only eight feet tall. A minor detail. Ten-foot-tall racks won't stand up in a room with an eight-foot ceiling!" Jim's voice was climbing.

Judy looked from the ceiling to the ten-foot-long wood brace in Jim's hand. "I'm sure the instructions said ten feet. I'll go look."

"What good does that do now?" Jim's frown matched the rasp of his voice. "There's nothing to be done but saw off these confounded boards and redrill the holes so I can screw in the crosspieces. That will only take all night."

And it did. Judy held the poles while Jim sawed. She measured for the new screw holes. She checked her instruction sheet and found she had read the number correctly, but the festival had changed locations. The trouble was that the organizer hadn't changed the instruction sheets. When the racks were finally in place, others pitched in and helped hang the quilts.

When the droopy-eyed couple arrived at the opening the next morning, the judges had already made their rounds and handed down their decisions.

"Judy, come here!" Jim called across the room.

Oh no, what's wrong now? she thought as she walked over, too tired to face another problem.

"Look!" Jim grabbed her at the waist and swung her around in circles as if she were a child. "You won. Your Sunbonnet Sue quilt won second place! There is justice in the world after all. Do you think the judges knew it was your husband who stayed up all night, making the display beautiful?" He put a finger on his chin.

"No! Now you're sleepy *and* dopey. There aren't any names on the quilts. Maybe an angel nudged the judges."

"Maybe you are just one good quilter."

"Maybe you're the best husband a quilter ever had."

The Master Pattern

From that day on, half of my men did the work, while the other half were equipped with spears, shields, bows and armor. The officers posted themselves behind all the people of Judah who were building the wall. Those who carried materials did their work with one hand and held a weapon in the other.

Nehemiah 4:16–17

Cooperation and teamwork hastened the Israelites' progress and prevented the enemy's stopping their building. By helping with one another's work, we thwart Satan's efforts to sabotage success. When we contribute to others' accomplishing projects and achieving goals, we experience doubled joy. In addition to rejoicing for the other person, we feel the same satisfaction as if it were our own accomplishment.

God, increase my willingness and my ability to help others succeed.

A Gratitude Quilt

"What are we supposed to do about a hurricane?" Carmen asked, her brown eyes wide with alarm as she listened to warnings on the radio.

"I don't know. I've never been in a hurricane in the United States before." Rosario dropped onto the mattress that rested on the floor.

Carmen sat close beside her mother and put her hands over her ears. "I wish the wind would stop. It's scary."

"Shhh. Don't worry your sisters." Rosario looked at her other two daughters playing with their rag dolls at a card table. The table served as a place to eat until the family earned enough money to purchase real furniture.

Arriving from Barcelona, Spain, only three months before, the Cirilo family was grateful for the little house, even if it was small and unfinished. It represented a toehold for a new life in America, the fulfillment of their dream.

"Mama, the wall is shaking!" Esma cried as she slid down from the card-table chair and ran to cuddle with her mother.

The whole family jumped when the door flew open, banging into the wall behind it, leaving a dent from the doorknob. Rafael blew in with the wind. The rain sweeping in with him nearly reached the mattress.

"Come on! Everyone into the truck!" Rafael ordered his family. "We must evacuate at once. The eye of the hurricane is expected to hit Port O'Connor. This house is too low if the water rises, and the wind is too strong for these thin walls." Rafael snatched jackets off the pegs by the door. The house shuddered as if to warn them to flee.

"Will the wind blow our house down?" Esma asked, clinging to her father's leg.

"I hope not."

Carmen grabbed the two rag dolls her sisters were playing with, scooped up Pia, and ran with the others to the truck. She leaned forward and pushed with all her might against the wind. She felt as if its blasts pinned her in place.

By the time they reached the school that was designated as the evacuation shelter for people from the low-lying areas, Carmen didn't know if she was shaking from the cold or from suffocating fear.

When the wind finally stopped, Carmen could still hear its roar in her head. Rafael and the other men left the shelter to check their homes.

Only a short time later, Carmen spotted her father as soon as he appeared in the gymnasium doorway. She knew, from the slump of his shoulders, that he didn't bring good news.

"The house is gone," Rafael said quietly, then wrapped his arms around Rosario and burrowed his head in the crook of her neck.

Gone. The word blasted the family as fiercely as the wind had. The girls' wails drew the stares of the school's other occupants.

Years later, what Carmen remembered most was a lady with a white vest bearing a big red cross on it. She appeared from nowhere and perched on the cot beside her mother. Carmen's distraught mind didn't take in any of the words, but the woman's soft tone of voice quieted her parents, and Carmen's heart resumed its normal beat. Within hours, the Red Cross had provided the family with a few changes of clothes. Within the week, its representatives had situated the family in a motel and provided vouchers to use in a grocery store. The "cross" lady, as Esma persisted in calling her, became a symbol of strength as they began again.

Every year after the hurricane, Rosario made a little cake and talked with her girls about their escape from the vengeance of the storm. One year, when everyone had outgrown the gift clothes from the Red Cross, Rosario announced a different celebration. "I don't ever want to forget how God sent us help after the hurricane. We'll make a quilt from the Red Cross clothes. Every time we look at it, we'll remember how the Lord used kind people to get us back on our feet again."

The girls enjoyed cutting Sunbonnet Sue hats and dresses from their storm clothes. When the quilt was finished, Rosario hung it on their living room wall, and every visitor

61

heard the story about God sending an angel of mercy, one wearing a Red Cross, to help poor immigrants.

The Master Pattern

Praise the LORD, O my soul,
  and forget not all his benefits—
who forgives all your sins
  and heals all your diseases,
who redeems your life from the pit
  and crowns you with love and compassion.

Psalm 103:2–4

Rosario found an interesting way to remember God's goodness to her family in a traumatic time. We don't need to make a quilt to memorialize God's faithfulness, but we do need to remember it. Think of his benefits for you and thank God for them every day.

Lord, thank you for all the kindnesses you shower on my life. Help me to remember your goodness in days gone by.

Lone Star

Although the Lone Star quilt, sometimes called the Star of Bethlehem, is firmly associated with the state of Texas, the first use of the pattern actually occurred in the 1830s, before the birth of the Republic of Texas. When Texas designed a flag using a one-star emblem, people thought of the Lone Star quilt as a symbol of the state. The precise matching of the Lone Star quilt pieces constitutes a difficult challenge. The seamstress must precisely cut, align, and stitch the center eight diamonds. Any mistake will multiply with each row, and as a consequence, the entire star will end up awry.

The same is true of our lives: If we "cut" and "match" each piece correctly, we will probably produce a wonderful result. If, however, we mismatch here or misshape there, we can still experience the beautiful threads of God's grace, making all well. These stories reflect the Father's mercy in broken as well as happy circumstances: A young man enters college full of family wisdom; a paralyzed man becomes a master quilter; an old quilt takes on new life; an elderly woman with failing eyesight still crafts works of art. With God's loving, though subtle, intervention, every outcome is perfect.

Homemade Values

"Bob, are you sure this is the cover you want as the spread for your bed?" Anna kept her voice low, in case Bob's college roommate came back with his next load of boxes to move into the freshman dorm.

"Yeah. I think it's cool Grandma made me a quilt for college."

"It's beautiful, for sure, but will the guys tease you about it?" Anna asked. Anna and Bob had met his roommate, Mitch, for the first time that morning when they arrived on campus to unpack Bob's things.

"Mom, it's a Lone Star quilt. It's not like it's loaded with bunnies or hearts and flowers."

"Still . . ." Anna stopped. She wanted Bob to get off to a good start with his dorm mates. She wasn't sure homemade quilts—stitched by Grandma, for goodness' sake—qualified as macho decor.

"Guys probably won't even notice what's on my bed. If they do, so what?" Bob took the quilt from his mother and unfolded it. "I'm sure enough proud of my state, and the Lone Star stands for Texas."

"I just don't want anyone to think you're too attached to your family or anything."

"Hey, I'm not ashamed of my family or my grandma. I'm proud of her. Here," Bob said, handing his mother one end of the quilt, "help me get the star in the center of the bed."

He stood back and smiled at his mother over the large red, white, and blue star that dominated the quilt's design. "What's all this, anyway? You're the one who taught me to stick to my values and not compromise to impress anyone."

Anna grinned, walked around the bed, and wrapped both arms around her tall son in a tight hug. "Looks like the student learned better than the teacher."

Bob led her in a little two-step dance. "I intend to remember the other part of what you drummed into my thick skull, too."

"What part is that?"

"It doesn't matter what people think. It matters what God thinks. I suspect I'll have lots of occasions to remind myself to figure out what God thinks and then stick to his viewpoint."

Anna relaxed. Bob's heart and mind were in the right place.

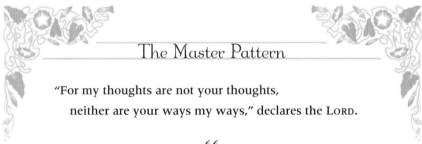

The Master Pattern

"For my thoughts are not your thoughts,
    neither are your ways my ways," declares the LORD.

"As the heavens are higher than the earth,
    so are my ways higher than your ways
and my thoughts than your thoughts."

Isaiah 55:8–9

So many important authorities and influences in our current society do not bother asking how God views an issue. Instead of forming opinions and choosing actions based on God's standards, people tend to weigh concepts and behavior via reasoning alone. God gave us brains to evaluate the world around us, but he wants us to subject our brain processes to his Word as the final authority.

God, show me your ways. Help me resist the temptation to measure by the world's standards instead of yours.

Thread for a Lifeline

"I didn't think things could get any worse," Hannah said, watching her brother, Zack, unload the used wheelchair from his wagon.

"Different, not worse, daughter," Bart corrected Hannah from the rocking chair on the low front porch of the farmhouse. "To tell the truth, I'm right glad to have that wheelchair. You wait and see. I'll sashay around here and get under your feet so much, you'll wish I wasn't so independent." Bart put his hands under his thigh and lifted it to shift his position. "Wheelchair or not, God's still in control."

"I hope he controls the cow's milk production. We're running out of food, the feed for the cows is low, and the medical bills keep piling up," Hannah remarked as Zack wheeled the chair up the front path.

"We'll pay 'em. Same way we paid for these cows in the first place." Bart waved toward the pasture where Guernsey

68

cows grazed. "Guess you were too young to remember how we got this herd."

Zack put the wheelchair next to his father, wedged his arms under his father's armpits, and with a grunt hoisted Bart up. Swiveling, Zack lowered him into the wheelchair.

"Ride 'em, cowboy!" Bart shouted. He spun the wheels of his chair, spurted forward, and nearly tumbled off the low lip of the porch.

"That's enough, Dad," Hannah said. "Tell us about those cows," she added, hoping to siphon off some of his exuberance.

Bart settled back. "It was right after the Spanish-American War. Those were hard days, in 1895."

Zack and Hannah sat on the porch swing to listen.

"The country sank into a depression. I worked seven days a week, twelve hours a day, for three years for our first cow. Second one didn't take quite as long, but it wasn't quick, either. Your ma and I, we established this dairy farm one cow at a time. And we didn't starve while we got it going, either. God sees to it his children eat bread." Remembering, Bart looked at the nearby cows munching grass and swishing the flies with their tails.

"That's how I'm gonna pay my doctor bills, too: one at a time. I reckon I'll just help myself to your scrap pile, daughter, and start making them pretty quilts like you make. We'll sell them and pay our bills."

True to his word, Bart threw himself into quilting with the same resolve he had employed to earn his cows. Using his knack for colors and his skill at piecing, he constructed beautiful comforters that sold well. When he entered his large Lone Star quilt in the Washington State Fair, he won first prize. His reputation established, he enjoyed travelers' visits to the farm to buy his quilts.

The Master Pattern

For every animal of the forest is mine,
and the cattle on a thousand hills.

Psalm 50:10

Usually, when God provides for his people, our hard work contributes to the process. To our surprise, the labor creates its own rewards: Work results in satisfaction and character growth. Sometimes God grants us unearned benefits; either way, we can trust him to care consistently for us. As Bart experienced, God supplied his need one cow at a time.

God, thank you for your provision. Help me trust you to meet all of my needs.

Worn but Not Worn Out

"You should throw away this worn-out old quilt. It's decrepit," Keith complained as he pulled the raggedy comforter out of the blanket chest and tossed it on the floor.

"I can't," Darlene answered, scooping the quilt off the floor. "My grandmother made it."

"Worthless, moth-eaten thing. Not worth the space it takes," her husband grumbled.

"She was more proud of this Lone Star quilt than any other one she made. I was just a little girl, but I remember her talking about how hard it was to align the pieces."

"Get rid of it. Will you ever tidy things up around here?" Kevin shoved a pile of magazines from a table onto the floor.

Will you ever stop grouching over every little thing? Darlene swallowed the retort and picked up the magazines. She put them in the wastebasket after separating a mail-order catalog from the pile.

"You might as well throw the catalog away, too. Don't you be asking for Christmas gift money for the grandchildren this year. The money isn't there." Keith picked up the catalog, added it to the wastebasket, and marched outdoors to the garbage can.

"And that's why we just had this crazy little flap: money," Darlene told Tiger, the cat. "Keith's moods always boil down to money." She sat on the sofa to ponder the grandchildren-gift edict Keith had delivered. "Lord, you say you can transform us until we reflect your glory. You have a long way to go with Keith and me." She ran her hands over the quilt as she prayed. The material in the big star that burst out of the middle of the quilt still looked beautiful. The worn-out appearance came from the threadbare fabric around it.

Just then, Tiger rolled over on her back and batted a Styrofoam ball that had escaped Darlene's craft basket.

"That's the answer," she said suddenly.

"What answer?" Keith asked, coming back in from his trash hauling.

"Money for gifts." Darlene pulled out her scissors and set to work. By the end of the week, she had cut the good parts of her great-grandmother's Lone Star quilt into pieces. With tiny stitches, she sewed quilted pieces together to fit tightly around large Styrofoam balls and attached yarn loops on one end. She had created some spectacular new Christmas tree ornaments.

To her delight, the ornaments brought a handsome sum when she took them to a silent auction at her office. Others put in orders for more. By the time she used up all the good parts of the quilt, Darlene was thrilled with the money in her Christmas fund. She kept out one ornament for each of her children as a memento of their great-great-grandmother.

Darlene invited Keith to go with her to buy a little gift for each grandchild. Together, they laughed over who would enjoy which toy. Keith even offered some extra money for the shopping spree.

At home, Darlene prayed, "I know we are a long way from reflecting your glory, Lord. But thanks for letting Keith and me enjoy a lighthearted evening, centered around the joy of giving."

The Master Pattern

And we, who with unveiled faces all reflect the Lord's glory, are being transformed into his likeness with ever-increasing glory, which comes from the Lord, who is the Spirit.

2 Corinthians 3:18

Darlene's inspiration turned an old, worn-out quilt into a fund-raiser and a set of keepsakes for her grandchildren. Nothing is so shabby that God can't transform it into something beautiful. He even enjoys tweaking our personalities until we gleam with his character. Until the day we die, God will mold us more and more into his likeness. Nothing is impossible for God; no one is beyond God's use in his kingdom.

Lord, please fashion good from the aspects of my life that appear worn and threadbare.

Sharp Eyes

As the teenager passed by the door to the family room, Miriam called, "Jimmy, come in here. I need your help."

Jimmy kept his face straight ahead, clutched his football more tightly, and walked by as if he had not heard. He knew what the old woman wanted.

When Kathy walked into the room to do homework on the computer, though, she couldn't ignore the request.

"My old eyes don't see well enough to thread needles anymore. Would you thread this for me?" Miriam held out her needle to Kathy.

Without trying to conceal a sigh of irritation, Kathy slipped the white thread into the tiny hole. Before she found the information she needed for her history paper, she had repeated the task for her grandma, with increasing annoyance, four more times.

After the last time, Miriam commented, "It's aggravating not to be able to thread my needles myself. Funny thing, I still see well enough to do the quilting, if someone else will just keep me in threaded needles." Her quick finger movements put a dozen tiny stitches in her Lone Star quilt before Kathy could sit back down at her desk.

Sudden concern filled Miriam's face. "My work does look okay, doesn't it?" She held her quilt out to Kathy. "Take a close look and see if my vision has affected my stitches."

Kathy got up again from the computer and looked at the quilt. "Your sewing looks great, Grandma. You know, people put their names on a waiting list to buy your beautiful quilts." Kathy held out the quilt. "I love how you arranged the colors from the yellow Lone Star center to deep red at the tip of each branch."

"Guess I still have an eye for color, but it's frustrating having to trouble others to thread my needles. Sometimes I have to sit here a long time with idle hands before someone comes by to thread them for me. I need to keep turning out quilts to help your dad. Pays for my keep, so to speak."

"Grandma! You don't have to worry about that," Kathy protested.

"I may not see a tiny needle hole so well, but my ears are as keen as ever. I know what I hear, and money's tight around here." Shaking her head, she added, "I don't want to be a troublesome old lady. And threading these needles is a nuisance to you busy young people."

"Grandma, we love you." Kathy threw her arms around her grandmother's thin shoulders. "You're not troublesome. I'm sorry we sometimes act impatient about threading your needles."

Kathy snapped her fingers. "I've got an idea! Let's buy a big package of needles. You make a list of how many needles you want threaded and with which colors. Jimmy and I can thread needles while we're watching television,

75

and we'll hardly know we're doing the job. We'll stick them in your pincushion, and the next day, you can sew without stopping." Kathy spread her arms wide in enthusiasm. "Good idea, huh?"

The system worked well. Without the long stretches of trying in vain to thread her own needles, or waiting on others, Miriam produced more quilts. Eventually, she earned enough to replace the worn vinyl flooring in the kitchen.

The Master Pattern

Again I tell you, it is easier for a camel to go through the eye of a needle than for a rich man to enter the kingdom of God.

Matthew 19:24

Kathy and Jimmy discovered that giving to God involved more than dropping money into the collection box at church. They found another way to enter into kingdom living was to inconvenience themselves to help others. Giving up time they wanted for themselves felt as difficult to them as giving money was for the rich man in the Scripture above.

Enlarge my concept of serving the kingdom of God. Help me to be willing to humble myself and make the sacrifices necessary to fulfill your plan for my life.

Ohio Star

Examples of the Ohio Star quilt exist from the early 1800s. Usually an Ohio Star quilt is not a medallion quilt but one that contains many stars placed in a pleasing arrangement. Sometimes quilters make it with a square surrounded by eight triangles, which form the branches of the stars.

In one of these stories, stars ignite a plan for freedom in an abused young woman; in another, quilted stars are the victims of bad judgment. The Ohio Star quilt reminds friends of an ill companion, and one made of a daddy's shirts wraps a little boy in comfort. Like God's amazing love, beautiful threads weave through all of our stars, quilted or real, and all of our stories.

Greasy Stitches

"Hold on," Paul said, tugging the chain around his car engine.

"Is pulling out your own car engine really worth all this sweat?" asked Chuck, who was holding the rope firmly with both hands. He wiped his head against his sleeve to absorb the moisture on his forehead before it dripped into his eyes.

"Sure is. The shop charges a fortune to remove an engine before overhauling it." Paul secured the chain.

"No wonder. It's a nasty job."

"A dirty one, for sure," Paul agreed, wiping his hands on a nearby rag. "You can let go now. I think the chain will hold. It's a good thing I can use Dad's truck while he's gone for training. The shop said there's a backup of business, so it'll be weeks before the mechanic gets to my job.

"Now I need to wrap the engine in something to protect it from the salty sea air near the shop." He looked around the garage. "This old blanket ought to do the trick." Paul picked up a quilt from the top of an open box in the garage.

"Good idea. You don't want to get grease all over your truck bed, either."

Paul spread the quilt in the back of the truck. Chuck backed the truck bed under the engine. Using a pulley, Paul lowered the engine on top of several blue and brown quilted stars. Wrapping the quilt around the oil-slicked engine, he tied it in place with a rope.

"Let's go." Paul passed a rag to Chuck. After wiping their blackened hands, they climbed in the truck to drive the engine to the shop for overhauling.

Several weeks later, Paul was cleaning spark plugs for his dad's truck when his mother came into the garage.

"Thanks for working on your dad's truck while he's gone." Grace threaded her way through tools, a lawn mower, and the shop vacuum to a stack of boxes. "Would you help me carry this top box to my car? I promised your Aunt Joan I'd bring her some of Great-Aunt Ada's things." She peered into the box. "Wait a minute. Where is Ada's Ohio Star quilt?"

Grace lifted up a quilted pillow and looked under some embroidered pillowcases. She saw nothing but some kitchen utensils and a couple of old books.

Paul stared at his mother.

"I know I put her Ohio Star quilt in the top of this box. I was still debating whether to keep it, but I decided the blue and brown stars went with Joan's color scheme better. This is where I put it."

Paul busied himself with the spark plugs. Grace kept muttering about the missing quilt, not noticing the red color washing Paul's face.

Once the engine was overhauled, Paul stuffed the greasy quilt as far back under his dad's workbench as he could. The filthy fate of Great-Aunt Ada's quilt wasn't discovered for years.

The Master Pattern

Do not give dogs what is sacred; do not throw your pearls to pigs. If you do, they may trample them under their feet, and then turn and tear you to pieces.

Matthew 7:6

Just like Paul didn't understand the value of a homemade quilt, people need a certain amount of knowledge to appreciate the work required to make a quilt. Without respect for the lengthy, detailed process, they may not understand the worth of a family quilt. In the same way, if people don't recognize the price Jesus Christ paid that we might be saved, to present them with the gospel over and over invites them to trample the message like the pigs in Matthew 7:6. With people who don't understand our enthusiasm and love for our Savior, a better approach is to offer them friendship without preaching. Once our lives intrigue them, they won't stomp and tear at the message of Christ; they will listen because of their esteem for us as friends.

God, help me to establish friendly relationships with people. Make my friendships point to Jesus Christ.

A Symbol of Hope

"Stay away from the door!" Jeb yelled.

"I just wanted to stand in the sunshine," Emma protested.

"I've told you time and again: You're to stay in the cabin." Jeb dropped the bar across the door into its metal brackets.

"Jeb, I'm not going anywhere," Emma said, her shoulders slumped.

"Other men might see you."

"Out here in the territories, there aren't a whole lot of men. Anyway, I'm your wife."

"And I'm older than you by twenty years." Jeb rubbed his hand over his gray hair. "Don't you get a notion to take up with some spry young man."

"I don't want another man. I just want to take little walks and talk to the woman in the next log cabin down the river," Emma pleaded.

"You got plenty to do right here in this cabin. No traipsing off for silly woman chatter. I'll tell you all you need to know."

Jeb plucked a caterpillar off his sleeve and flicked it into the cooking fire. "The caterpillars are wearing extra-wooly skin this summer. Means there's a cold winter coming. You best get to making another quilt before the winter sets in."

Grateful the caterpillar had sidetracked Jeb's wrath, Emma checked the fabric scraps in her basket. She fingered some pretty blue fabric, a gift from the lady in the nearest log cabin. She had brought the material when Emma arrived as Jeb's mail-order bride. But even calico in her favorite color couldn't overcome Emma's despair and stir any inspiration to design a quilt. Jeb was right, though, about needing another quilt. She shivered at the memory of the wind whistling between the chinks in the cabin logs last winter.

Long after Jeb fell asleep on the straw mattress beside her, Emma lay awake, rubbing the bruise on her arm from when Jeb had grabbed her out of the doorway. She used to think night was the hardest time, when she felt as if her isolation threatened her very sanity. Then she discovered that the biggest chink between the logs in her cabin was beside her bed. When she sat cross-legged, her eyes were at the right level to look out the crack. She looked forward to clear, starry nights. She waited until Jeb was snoring beside her, then, cushioning herself with her pillow, she put her face up to the crack and looked out at the stars. They stretched out over the fields and forests, twinkling as if beckoning her to join them.

A star led the wise men to Jesus, **Emma thought.** *After the wise men found him, God warned them not to return to Herod, because he wanted to harm the Christ child. God helped Jesus escape.* To Emma, as she peeked between the chinks, the sky became a map calling her to freedom. "Jesus, bring your light into my dark world," she whispered.

Now she knew what she would quilt. Her mother had taught her the Ohio Star pattern when she was a child. She'd cut out the blue fabric and stitch stars to help her remember that God was in his heaven, and he would help her in her troubles.

"Hear my prayer, O God," she murmured too loud.

Jeb's snore became a snort, and he sat up in bed, throwing an arm out to find her in the dark. "What are you up to, woman, peering out of the logs? You plotting a way out of here?" Jeb's fist connected with her right eye and flattened her back onto the bed. Fastening his hand around her wrist, he snarled, "You took a vow, and you aren't going anywhere."

And you took a vow to love and cherish me, Emma thought, tenderly feeling around her bruised eye.

Emma found comfort in piecing her Ohio Star quilt. With each point she attached to the star's square center, she thought about the wide, endless sky and imagined herself walking away under the cover of darkness. When the quilt was finished, she wrapped a few garments and her mother's ivory comb in it and laid it aside, waiting.

One crisp fall day, Jeb was working in the back, butchering hogs. Emma took the bundle, slipped out the door, and darted from tree to tree until she was out of sight of the cabin. Staying off the trail, she ran past the first log house down the river. It was too close to ask for refuge. She ran on past the second cabin. Whenever she felt she couldn't run any farther, she thought how often the Psalms talked of God giving strength. She finally came to a pier, where a man poled a raft carrying wagons and people across the river.

The bearded man's searching stare took in her black eye and bruised arm. Reaching for her elbow, he helped her board the raft, never mentioning a charge for his ferry service.

As she watched the far riverbank approach, Emma clutched her Ohio Star quilt and began to believe she could find freedom from the life she had led. When they reached the village across the river, she would ask directions to a church.

The Master Pattern

God is our refuge and strength,
an ever-present help in trouble.

Psalm 46:1

God is faithful to provide us strength for every need. He also understands the limits of our endurance and is a safe haven in times of trouble, no matter how desperate. His help is only as far away as the cries of our hearts.

God, I'm coming to you as my refuge from the difficulties of my life. Strengthen me in them and reveal your help for me.

The Tie That Binds

"I wish Berta were here," Megan said, standing with her friends in front of an Ohio Star quilt hung at the quilt festival in Nashville, Tennessee.

"Me, too. The Ohio Star pattern is one of her favorites. She cried on the phone when she told me her doctor wouldn't let her come." Jody choked at the memory. "She wanted to see her German quilting friends in the worst way. 'One last time' were her words."

"I wish we'd thought up the idea of having a reunion of our overseas quilting guild last year. She probably could have come. It's been so long since those wonderful days of sewing together at the base in Germany." Megan hugged the quilter closest to her. "I guess we've all missed each other."

"And become better quilters, judging from the wall hangings we made," Gretchen said. "I'm amazed to see how differently we all used the same pieces of fabric."

"I'm glad we mailed them to each other as far ahead of time as we did," Jody said, cheering up at the thought. "It took me forever to figure out what design to put together."

"As sick as Berta's been since the cancer remission ended, I was surprised she still made her quilt hanging from the pieces we passed around," Gretchen said.

"That reminds me: How are we going to quilt the hand-print squares we brought with us for Berta? We need the quilt done in time for you to take it to Berta in Florida on your way back to Germany, Gretchen."

"Can I help you ladies quilt something?" asked a man demonstrating his quilting machine in the booth behind them.

"Wish we could afford one of those fancy machines. We'd have our friend's quilt done in a flash," Megan answered, longing showing in her face.

"A sick friend, am I right?" the man asked.

"Cancer," Jody said. "She was supposed to join us here, but she's too sick. We want to send her a quilt to tell her we love her."

"Bring it to me. I'll quilt it." The man's face crinkled with his smile.

"Are you serious?" Megan asked, her eyebrows raised.

"I have to demonstrate this machine all day, every day of this festival. I might as well demonstrate it on a gift to your sick friend."

They all stared at the man who made the unbelievably kind offer.

Thanks to his help, the quilt, along with photos of each of their wall hangings and every Ohio Star quilt displayed at the festival, was ready to send by the time they left. Best of all, each handprint on the quilt carried a message of love to a needy friend.

The Master Pattern

Keep your lives free from the love of money and be content with what you have, because God has said,

"Never will I leave you;
never will I forsake you."

Hebrews 13:5

The ladies who quilted together at the military base in Germany developed a love for one another that bridged their later geographic separation. Knitted together by a common interest, they maintained contact for years. God is infinitely more faithful than people. He never drops his connection to us. His interest in us is all-encompassing, and his support is never ending.

Thank you, God, for your faithfulness to me. Help me be a reliable friend.

Quilt Comfort

"I can't sleep, Mama," Caleb said, his voice trembling. "I need to sleep in your bed."

Sandra opened her eyes, puffy from bouts of crying, to see her six-year-old clutching his threadbare teddy at her bedside. Too exhausted to speak, Sandra pulled back the covers. Caleb climbed in and cuddled next to her. She rubbed his back until he drifted off to sleep. Sandra tossed, unable to doze off herself.

The next morning, she stood with the other mothers waiting for the school bus to pick up their children. "If the grief doesn't destroy us, lack of sleep will. How long is it okay to allow Caleb to sleep in my bed since his dad died?" Sandra asked her neighbor.

"Is he still unable to sleep in his own room?" Peggy slipped a sympathetic arm around her friend's waist.

"It's been only a month since Dan died, and I understand my son's grief. Mine feels raw and fresh. Still, I wonder if it's healthy for Caleb to sleep in my bed. Not to mention that I'm exhausted from interrupted sleep, which only adds to my ragged emotions."

By the time the bus pulled away and the neighbors called good-bye, drifting back toward their houses, Peggy had an idea. "Have you cleaned out your husband's clothes yet?"

"No. I guess I should, but I keep putting it off. It makes his death seem so final." Sandra gave a wry smile. "As if every moment of the day doesn't remind me of the finality of our loss."

"How about if I come and help you sort through his shirts? I was thinking I could make a quilt out of them, and Caleb could sleep with it. Maybe that would help him with his grief and keep him in his own bed."

"You would do that?" Sandra asked, hugging her friend. "Maybe cleaning the closet would go better with you there. I'm so tired of the constant crying. I just can't stop since Dan died."

Sorting through Dan's closet was hard, and Peggy's presence didn't eliminate the wrenching sense of loss. But Sandra felt an element of healing in finishing the job. Somehow it seemed to help her face forward, look to the future. She welcomed Peggy's help in deciding what were keepsakes for Caleb and what to do with everything else.

Sandra was surprised when, only a month later, Peggy arrived on her doorstep with a large package under her arm.

"Is that a present for me?" Caleb asked, eyeing the wrapping paper around Peggy's large bundle.

"How did you guess?" Peggy set the package on the coffee table. "It's a very special gift for you."

After tearing off the wrapping paper, Caleb looked bewildered. "A blanket?"

"It's not just any old blanket," Peggy said. "It's an Ohio Star quilt. And it's made out of the shirts your daddy wore. When you wrap up in this blanket, you can feel very close to your dad. You can pretend he's hugging you as he used to when he wore these shirts."

"Look, Caleb," Sandra said, pointing. "This brown-checked material is from the shirt Daddy wore to take you fishing, and here's the shirt Daddy often wore to church."

"This looks like the shirt with flowers Daddy bought in Florida," Caleb said as he pulled the quilt into his arms and laid his cheek on it.

"Now you can sleep in your own bed with a quilt that feels like a daddy-hug." Peggy smiled at Caleb.

"Remember how we talked about God as your heavenly Father?" Sandra asked. "When you cover up with this quilt, you can remember that God is holding you in his hug and looking after you."

"It smells like Daddy." Caleb smiled and took a big sniff.

That night, snuggled in his blanket, Caleb found comfort and began to sleep in his own bed again.

The Master Pattern

I will not leave you as orphans; I will come to you.

John 14:18

Caleb's quilt was a tangible reminder of his father, but Caleb's mother helped him see it as a reminder that God watched over him. God's presence is always available to help us conquer grief. His love surrounds us through the thoughtful gestures of people like Peggy. If we ask, God will help us recognize his comfort in the touchable love of those near us. He will also grant us a sense of his nearness and his great love for us. Although we can't see or feel him with our natural senses, he brings a peace that is beyond our understanding.

God, send your Holy Spirit to speak comfort to the depth of my being, in the circumstances that grieve my heart.

Grandmother's Fan

The attractive, fan-shaped arrangement of carefully blended color wedges became extremely popular in the late nineteenth century. Perhaps this was because the pattern's numerous wedges allowed the seamstress to put her scraps of leftover fabric to beautiful use. In more affluent homes, quilters sometimes cut the wedges from silk.

Silk roses, pricey fabric, a mystery quilt, and indigo cakes: These are the ingredients in stories about Grandmother's Fan quilts, confidence, friendship, God's love, and American history. Beautiful threads, both literal and figurative, result from each lesson learned—in the stories and in our own lives.

A Gift That Will Last

"For me?" Patty asked, her voice rising in surprise.

"You're the best quilting teacher ever, and you deserve a rose corsage," Renee said as she pinned the pink rosebuds to the collar of Patty's blue dress.

"Bright, artistic students make any teacher look good." Patty hugged Renee, being careful not to squash the corsage. "I still can't believe you wanted to have a luncheon for me."

"It's about time. By my count, you've been teaching quilting classes for at least fifteen years. Look around at all the beauty your instruction has inspired." Renee waved her arm toward the walls of the fellowship hall. Quilts and wall hangings of many sizes and patterns hung as a lovely tribute to a beloved teacher. The Grandmother's Fan quilt was most prevalent, since everyone in Patty's last class had learned that design.

By the time the casserole dishes were empty and the cookie platters held only crumbs, Patty felt as sated with appreciation as she did with the food. She thought her face must be shining with pleasure as brightly as the silver-engraved plaque was gleaming in the candlelight of the banquet tables.

Arriving home, she hung the silver plaque on an empty hook in her hall and tucked the program brochure into her scrapbook, ready to mount when she'd had her pictures of the event developed. "You should have seen it, Tabby," she told the orange-and-white cat rubbing against her leg. "Everybody cooked her best recipe, and we ate until we couldn't eat another bite."

She bent to pat her cat. "There weren't any chicken legs, or I would have brought you one. You'll have to make do with a spoonful of cat food." She grabbed a spoon, opened the refrigerator, retrieved a half-empty can, and placed a morsel in front of Tabby. She earned purring thanks for the snack.

"You're welcome, Tabby. While I'm at it, I'll put my corsage in here, next to your breakfast. That'll remind me to wear it to church Sunday, if it's still nice." Patty took off her flowers and put them gently in a plastic baggie, careful not to touch the blossoms and risk turning them brown. She put the corsage on the refrigerator shelf.

Sunday morning, she still felt the afterglow from the praise heaped on her at her pupils' luncheon. She pulled her corsage out of the refrigerator, along with the cat food for Tabby, who always showed up whenever the fridge door creaked open.

"Still looking good, Tabby." Patty pulled out the corsage. After she pinned it on, she began to giggle. "Tabby, guess what? These are *silk* roses. Here I've gone and refrigerated fake flowers! My quilting students will know I'm daft now." She laughed so hard she plopped down in a kitchen chair to catch her breath.

The Master Pattern

Give her the reward she has earned,
and let her works bring her praise at the city gate.

Proverbs 31:31

When Patty gave her time and talent to teach other women how to construct beautiful quilts, her contribution to their joy was greater than a material gift. Each student found a satisfying way to bless others at the same time she was discovering her own well of creativity. Therefore, the women wanted to express their appreciation to Patty with flowers that would last.

When we dedicate our gifts and talents to God, he will show us ways to share our skills with others. Ideally, we strive to leave the reward of our talents up to God. Our greatest compensation comes when our abilities bring praise to God, not to ourselves.

Lord, thank you for the abilities you have allowed me to develop. Help me use them to bring praise to you.

Warmth to Cover Icy Fear

"I'm glad I persuaded you to stop by Frances Fabric before you take me to your church service. I've never seen such elegant material," Shelly said, fingering a shimmering bolt of mauve fabric.

"I've never seen such expensive material," said Cara, her eyebrows raised at the price tag attached to it.

"This gold-flecked floral is a perfect match for my bedroom wallpaper. I've looked and looked for the right color combinations to make a quilt for my bed." Shelly spread a length of cloth on the counter.

"You'd better look again. Check out the price."

"I'm trying not to. I'll ignore the cost and indulge myself."

Cara regarded the stop at the fabric store on the way to church an easy bribe to lure Shelly into finally agreeing to attend services with her. She decided she'd better not say anything more about the cost while she waited for Shelly to pay for the extravagant material. Maybe Shelly's delight in her find would put her in a receptive mood to hear the minister at the evening service.

To Cara's disappointment, Shelly didn't respond to the altar call. At the beginning of the invitation, Shelly tried to hide her watery eyes by keeping her head down. After a while, though, the struggle within her created an overflow of tears, and her back began to shake with sobs.

"If you want to go forward and give your heart to God, I'll go with you," Cara whispered.

"I can't. I want to belong to God, but I can't."

"Why not? He loves you."

"I'd just let him down the way I let everyone down. I failed miserably when I was a teenager. I can't take a chance on failing again."

Cara offered a tissue, and Shelly blew her nose.

"God understands our failures. We don't clean ourselves up for him to accept us." Cara's voice rose in pitch. "He's the one who cleans us up. He wants you in whatever condition you will come."

"I can't. The cost is too high. No one in my family would understand."

Fear won. Nothing Cara said could reassure Shelly. Concerned for her friend, Cara dropped by her house more often.

"Started the quilt yet?" Cara asked each time she came to visit.

"Not yet," Shelly answered. "I'm afraid I'll cut it wrong. I can't risk a mistake at twenty dollars a yard. I don't want to waste the money."

"Shelly, you waste it if the material just sits in your cupboard, never used."

"I know. But every time I get it out, I feel almost paralyzed. It has to turn out right, or I've lost so much money."

With a flash of insight, Cara saw a connection to Shelly's misery at church. "Remember the night you listened to the altar invitation? You couldn't go and accept Jesus because you were afraid the price of becoming a Christian was too high. You feared you'd fail to do everything you thought a Christian should. Now fear is stopping you from enjoying a lovely quilt in your bedroom."

"I don't see how a quilt is like an altar call."

"It isn't," Cara agreed. "But fear is the enemy keeping you from acting in both instances. Let's look at some Bible verses together."

Later, asking God to take over her life, Shelly began her journey toward trust in him. As she grew to know God, she learned that his forgiveness covers every imperfection. And she began the Grandmother's Fan quilt she had longed to make.

The Master Pattern

But now, this is what the LORD says—
he who created you, O Jacob,
he who formed you, O Israel:
"Fear not, for I have redeemed you;
I have summoned you by name;
you are mine."

Isaiah 43:1

Surely God is my salvation;
   I will trust and not be afraid.
The LORD, the LORD, is my strength and my song;
   he has become my salvation.

Isaiah 12:2

Trusting God is the antidote to fear. When we realize he has redeemed us from our failures and is the source of our strength to overcome future difficulties, we can begin to trust God and overcome fear. Memorize these verses to say to yourself when you are afraid.

God, I lay my fears before you. Make me strong to overcome them.

Learning, Stitch by Stitch

"I'm never going to learn all those complicated computer programs," Hayley groaned as Mr. Gray slapped three thick manuals on her desk. "Which one should I study first?"

"As a secretary in this firm, you need to understand all our software." The growl in Mr. Gray's voice prohibited any further protest.

Then I quit, Hayley thought as her supervisor marched away. But she couldn't. Someone had to pay the mortgage on her house, and that someone was her since Alec had left. In addition to a broken heart, her ex-husband had left her with a broken furnace and a broken transmission in her car.

"Learning new programs is a bit overwhelming, isn't it?" Krista said cheerfully when she stopped by Hayley's desk with a smile of encouragement.

"That's an understatement! I need an emergency transfusion of computer knowledge. I can barely stumble around in Microsoft Word, let alone these other software programs." Hayley threw up her hands. "These manuals could be written in Greek for all I understand."

"Ask me if you have questions. You'll catch on fast." Krista patted Hayley's shoulder.

After several weeks of trying to learn the software and meet her boss's expectations, Hayley felt as if an entire orchestra percussion section were playing a concert inside her head. Her posture grew rigid with tension.

"Hayley, you need a hobby, something to relieve the stress," Krista remarked as she put a cup of hot tea on her friend's desk. "Come with me to my quilting guild tonight. We have a good time laughing and stitching."

Desperate for distraction from her job, Hayley agreed.

After the evening of exclaiming over beautiful colors and intricate patterns, Hayley signed up to participate in making a mystery quilt.

"Uh, Hayley, have you ever quilted before? In a mystery quilt, you aren't told what pattern you're sewing, so you only discover the design after you've completed quilting the pieces together. You have to follow the instructions exactly to make it come out properly. Some mystery quilts are complicated," Krista said, reluctant to discourage the enthusiasm she saw in her friend.

"I'll learn as I go."

"That's for sure." Krista wondered if she was doing her work friend a favor after all.

The mystery quilt turned out to have a Grandmother's Fan pattern that alternated squares of pinwheels, parallelograms, and stars.

"I think I'm ripping out one stitch for every one I succeed in getting right," said Hayley, giggling with Krista over her quilting adventures. "The fans look pretty, but the points don't quite come together. At least economic survival doesn't hang in the balance, though."

Krista laughed. "Just appliqué a circle over the points. No one will know the difference."

Hayley did and found her project relaxing. "Doesn't look half bad for a beginner. I'll just crunch it up on the back of my sofa and dare anyone to look for the faults!" Hayley laughed. "I'd like to dare Mr. Grim Gray when he looks for mistakes. If it weren't for the undo button on the computer, I'd probably be on the street by now."

"Maybe, but you're a lot more relaxed at the job since you've been sewing your quilt."

"I think stretching myself to learn all those fancy patterns in the mystery quilt changed my approach to undertaking something new. Somehow it seems more like an adventure than something with the power to destroy me."

"I never told you," Krista admitted, "that this year's mystery quilt is the hardest one we've ever done. Anything from now on should be a breeze."

To Hayley's relief, she felt less panic every time she encountered something new at her job after she conquered the mystery quilt.

The Master Pattern

You, dear children, are from God and have overcome them, because the one who is in you is greater than the one who is in the world.

1 John 4:4

When Hayley conquered a new hobby, the self-assurance she experienced carried over to help her master the skills needed in her new job. As Christians, we gain confidence from our knowledge that the Creator of the universe lives within us. The God mighty enough to set the sun in the skies, the God whose power determines the ebb and flow of the oceans—that God resides in our hearts. Whether our enemy is without, desiring to destroy us, or within the twists of our thinking, God is greater than our foe. He actually is within us to overcome our problems.

God, build my confidence in you. Build my abilities to overcome difficulties.

Indigo Days

"If only our crops hadn't failed last year as well as in 1873, you wouldn't have to get ready for work when the rich boys across town are getting ready for bed and tomorrow's school day." Billy's mother handed him a tin dinner pail with nourishment for his all-night watch at Mr. Strauss's dye company.

"Never mind, Ma. I don't like sitting closed up inside school, but I do like my job with Uncle Kenneth." Billy tried to cheer up his mother. "He says having someone my age is a good influence over the men's language. And you'll be proud when I bring you cakes of blue dye," Billy called out as he walked out the door. "Wait till you see what pretty blue colors you can use to dye your material for the Grandmother's Fan quilt you want to sew."

To Billy's delight, this night provided the highlight of his watch. "Wake up! The buds are about to bloom," he shouted, running into the office of Levi Strauss to rouse the slumbering man and his staff. The imperative moment had arrived for cutting the leaves from the bushes to make indigo dye. The men had to harvest the leaves at the last second before blooms burst forth.

Billy clapped a hand over his ears at the language the men used to express their irritation over their wake-up call.

"Can I watch for the greenish color?" Billy pestered his uncle after the leaves were cut. He loved being around the big vats of water full of leaves, steeping until they fermented and turned the water to a green color. Before long, Uncle Kenneth handed him a paddle.

Mr. Strauss measured a little limewater into the vat. "Okay, Billy, beat the mixture until it thickens. Today I'll send you home with a lighter blue dye for your ma's fabric. She'll be the envy of her quilting friends at the county fair."

Mr. Strauss studied fabric swatches. "Stop beating before the green water gets too dark. We're aiming for a lighter blue color."

Foul language poured along with the fluid when the men drew the water off the vats, taking care not to stir up the sediment at the bottom. But the sight of the boy with his hands on his hips hushed the men.

With hands and faces smudged blue from forming cakes of the sediment, the men joined Billy in a checker game while they waited for the dye cakes to dry in the shade. "It's not nice to make fun of someone," Billy scolded the others when they taunted a losing player.

Arriving home, Billy called to his mother, "Come see what I've got." Proudly he laid cakes of the new light blue dye onto the table next to darker blue ones. "You'll win the prize for the prettiest Grandmother's Fan quilt at the next fair. By the way, I've noticed the men stop swearing around me, and that's a relief."

Mother hugged him.

The Master Pattern

So then, let us not be like others, who are asleep, but let us be alert and self-controlled.

1 Thessalonians 5:6

Set a guard over my mouth, O LORD;
keep watch over the door of my lips.

Psalm 141:3

As long as Levi Strauss made indigo dye, Billy knew he could earn money. Mr. Strauss said, "The color is as good as gold." Billy's patience in watching outmatched that of every one of the workers, and he excelled in another way as well: He wasn't shy about correcting the men who were careless with their language. Besides refraining from profanity, we need to watch the impact of our words on others. Are we kind? Do we use words to manipulate? Do we gossip? Let us be alert to how our conversation affects others and use self-control in our dialogue.

Lord, set a guard over my mouth, so I will be careful with what I say and not harm anyone.

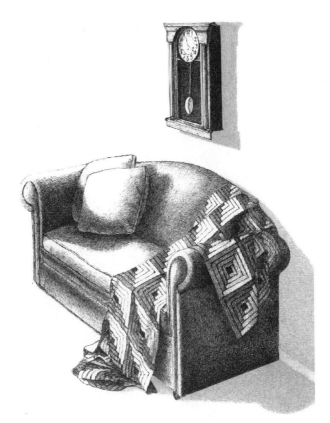

Log Cabin

Swedish settlers brought the log-home style to America when they started the New Sweden settlement in the Delaware River Valley in 1638. The Log Cabin quilt was named after this simple dwelling. Quilters often choose red for the center square of the design, which can furnish a place for embroidery and signatures. By careful arrangement of dark and light fabrics, the quilter can form zigzags, diamonds, or a square pattern called Barn Raising.

In this section, Log Cabin quilts and cloth, needles and nerves, fabric and friends, form the backdrops of stories. The tales remind us of the plight of less-fortunate folk, our need for endurance in disturbing days, how precious a single tool can be, and the way a hobby can calm a troubled mind or make a salve for fractured relationships. God's supplying our needs, by his own actions or those of his sensitive followers, remains constant; we have only to look for the beautiful threads of his faithfulness, for they are always there.

Cold Wind, Warm Quilt

"Finished!" April pulled her needle from the Log Cabin quilt and held it up with a flourish. "We did it."

"A monumental accomplishment, that's what I call it." Bethany reached for one end of the quilt and helped Alice fold it.

"Making one hundred quilts for the homeless shelter is no small achievement," Alice agreed. She looked around the church fellowship hall. "All of you ladies have a right to feel proud."

"Especially when we heard about the bad winter storm approaching, and we decided to push up our deadline to finish," Kim added. "Let's pack these in the back of the van and get them delivered to the housing quarters before the storm arrives. If it snows as much as predicted, I won't want to be on the roads in a few hours."

Alice's teeth were chattering by the time she started unloading the quilts at their destination. "I believe the weatherman was right when he said we'd set a record for subzero temperatures."

While the ladies finished unloading the quilts and ham biscuits, the shelter was already crowding with people fleeing the arctic air. The colorful Log Cabin quilts cushioned children napping on the floor. Bethany stopped to tuck a bare foot into the quilt cocoon one little boy had wound around himself. His thumb slipped out of his sleeping mouth at the additional warmth.

Alice carried the tray of ham biscuits and marveled at how fast a small child could swallow one.

Kim walked about, wrapping quilts around the shivering shoulders of worried mothers.

"You must be a quilt angel."

"It's as pretty as it is warm."

"Can I keep it?" asked one girl. She looked to be about ten, although she was so skinny, Alice couldn't be sure. "I never saw such a pretty one."

"Me, too, can I keep the blanket?" A young boy with a torn T-shirt sat cross-legged and wrapped in the quilt.

Another child took up the chorus, rubbing her cheek against the red, white, and blue material.

Alice looked at the director of the homeless shelter. The shelter's rules required all bedding to stay on the premises for use again and again. The director began, "Our policy . . ."

Alice didn't let the woman escape her stare.

"Well, this is an unusual storm," the director said, turning to see Kim and Bethany straighten and give her pointed looks. "You ladies made the blankets, so I guess we can let you decide the rules this one time."

"Yes, you can keep them," Alice said, looking into the deep brown eyes of the fragile boy beside her.

112

"Yeah!" The boy grabbed her around the knees with his thin arms. In a moment, hugging arms surrounded all three of the ladies.

By the time they climbed into the van, the snow was blowing ferociously across their windshield. "God, you provided for those poor people. Provide us with a safe drive back home," Alice prayed.

The Master Pattern

I was young and now I am old,
yet I have never seen the righteous forsaken
or their children begging bread.

Psalm 37:25

God is our Provider. Whether it is ham biscuits, cozy quilts, or a timely hug, God uses his power to bring his children what they most need. Sometimes we don't recognize that it was God who supplied, and sometimes we wait longer than we want for his provision. But if we continue to align ourselves with his righteousness, we will experience his deliverance. Our gracious God also enjoys supplying those who follow him with many of their desires in addition to meeting their needs.

Lord, help me recognize that you are my Provider. Thank you for your unfailing care, which so often goes beyond needs to include many of my wants.

Under-the-Table Cloth

"Spin your flax, Merry," Faith admonished her daughter. "I know we're weary of meeting our daily quota of spinning thread, but we can still rejoice. We'll have cloth in spite of the Navigation Acts." Faith adjusted her apron to cover a hole in her skirt, then resumed peeling potatoes.

"I can't rejoice when I could be thrown into prison for using a spinning wheel," Merry moaned, pulling her wheel farther back into the shadows of the room.

"I take comfort that our Massachusetts leaders, not just us all on our own, defied the English Navigation Acts. I'm glad our colony passed laws saying we must spin." Faith peeled another potato. "If there's any arresting done, I daresay it's our leaders the English will arrest. Meantime, we have cloth."

"Dutch ships used to bring prettier material to our ports than what we weave," Merry said. Her fingers worked the flax while her foot kept the spinning wheel going.

"But the only cost for our homemade material is our labor."

Merry made a face. "Our mother country doesn't behave very motherly, insisting that all our imports must first go to England. For added insult, she taxes them beyond reason."

Faith stirred peeled potatoes into the stew simmering in the pot hanging over the fire. "Your father thinks England's goal is to put the Dutch mercantile ships out of business."

"The country seems determined to make our lives in the colonies miserable." Merry stretched her legs at the spinning wheel. "It scares me when Grandfather makes his forbidden spinning wheels. If he's caught, the English customs office could order his hand cut off." She shuddered. "Do you think they'd really do such a terrible thing?"

"Sometimes I wake up with nightmares about the British Custom officers bursting through our doors and confiscating our spinning wheel," Faith admitted.

"It's not fair to make weaving our own cloth illegal, and at the same time to tax imported cloth so much," Merry complained.

"The British do seem to want all trade riches for themselves. Poor Uncle Enoch writes that he wants to come to America, but because he's trained in textiles, the authorities won't let him come."

"Shhh, you'll make Grandmother cry." Merry glanced toward the window, but her grandma was dozing over her knitting and didn't hear about her son's disappointment.

Merry tried a different topic in case the old woman woke up: "We still don't have enough material to make quilts for my marriage dowry."

"That's why I'm saving every scrap, even the little ones. The Log Cabin pattern requires only narrow, straight pieces. By the time Seth figures out you are the prettiest girl in the village and comes a-courting, I'll have a pretty quilt finished."

Merry said nothing but sped up her spinning.

The Master Pattern

Endure hardship with us like a good soldier of Christ Jesus.

2 Timothy 2:3

At the same time colonists endured the deprivations the English Navigation Acts caused, they became inventive in devising new tools and ways to supply their needs. As uncomfortable as hardships are at the time they occur, we often look back on them and realize they were times of personal growth. If we regard difficulties as an instrument of learning, we can find the strength to substitute creative thinking for complaining. God brings good out of trials by turning us into good soldiers equipped to serve him. He helps us grow.

Lord, let my trials increase my spiritual life.

The Lost Needle

"Penny!" Ernestine called her daughter. "Marabel sent word with your pa that she wants to use the settlement's needle. She's finishing up a Log Cabin quilt for Charity's wedding next month. Pa says the Whites are in a tizzy of activity getting ready for it. I'm turning our wood ashes into lye for our soap making, and I can't go. Soap will make a nice wedding present, don't you think?" Ernestine asked as she wove the needle into a scrap of black wool and handed it to her child. "Don't you loiter, Penny. Marabel's so eager to finish the quilt, she said she'd be tempted to pay the peddler for a needle if he were to come through the valley. Of course, he was here only six months ago and isn't due for another six months." Ernestine shook her head. "As if Marabel could afford a needle if he did come. As if any of us could. We'd not be sharing one needle amongst the lot of us if we had the money to buy one.

"Take care you don't drop it," she admonished her daughter. "Neighbor Brown wants it next, so she can hem some dish towels for her wedding gift."

"I'll go straight there, Mama." Penny left with Butch, the family mutt, close behind her. She felt important doing a significant errand. She knew to follow the trail through the woods between her pa's land stake and the Whites's holdings. When the trees dimmed the sunlight, she called Butch close and hurried her steps.

Without warning, Butch planted himself in front of her and stopped. A low growl came from deep in his throat. Penny saw his black hair bristle.

"What is it, boy?" She was reaching to pet the dog when she heard something crashing through the underbrush. Barking, Butch ran forward. At the sight of a shadowy form, Penny turned and ran toward her house.

When she burst through the door, Ernestine asked, "How did you manage to deliver the needle so fast?"

"I didn't," Penny gasped. "Something spooked Butch. Maybe it's a bear."

Butch ran up and Ernestine sighed. "Your imagination is too active. I'll just take the needle myself," she said, reaching for the piece of wool.

Penny looked down. She didn't have the needle.

Before the sun had time to sink, Penny's father ran to the tiny village schoolhouse and rang the bell in its steeple. The small community soon gathered to find out the nature of the emergency.

Everyone abandoned his or her chores to search for the precious needle.

Sobbing with regret, Penny showed them where she thought she heard the bear. When the men identified bear footprints in the soft soil, Ernestine threw her arms around her daughter. "Oh, Penny, better to lose our needle than our little girl."

On their hands and knees, the women separated the grass blades in their search for the needle, and the men scoured the woods with their rifles, looking for the bear. "The next time we take the needle from place to place, we'll put it in red cloth so it will show up better," Ernestine declared.

The Master Pattern

What do you think? If a man owns a hundred sheep, and one of them wanders away, will he not leave the ninety-nine on the hills and go to look for the one that wandered off? And if he finds it, I tell you the truth, he is happier about that one sheep than about the ninety-nine that did not wander off.

Matthew 18:12–13

Just as the community was determined to find its only needle, Jesus Christ is eager to save each of us. When a lost soul accepts Jesus, the joy in heaven is far greater than the party of celebration the small settlement had when one of its members found the precious needle.

God, help me carry your message of salvation to lost people in my neighborhood.

Stitches That Soothe

Brooke stopped in the middle of her dining room, surprised to find herself twisting a paper in her hands as if she were trying to make a knot out of it. *Calm down, Brooke,* she told herself and broke off her pacing to flop down on the sofa beside her husband in the family room.

"Have you worn out the carpet yet?" Tyler asked.

"What do you mean?" Brooke answered, evading his question.

"You've established quite a circuit since dinner. Down the hall, through the kitchen and dining room, back through the living room, and down the hall again. Round and round she goes, and when she'll stop, nobody knows."

Brooke swatted at his arm. "I didn't realize I was doing that."

"Relax, honey." Tyler put his arm around his wife and planted a kiss on the top of her head. "Lots of people are getting laid off from their jobs these days. It's not a disgrace."

120

Tyler wiped the tear that started down her cheek with his thumb. "Hey, we still have each other. We have our health. We'll get along. We'll tighten our belts a little. Before long, you'll find another position with a boss who appreciates all your wonderful talents and great insights."

"That's just it. Where did my insight fail? I could kick myself for not seeing this coming. Why didn't I get out and find another job before they gave me the ax?" Choking back tears, Brooke continued in a ragged voice, "I keep asking myself, What could I have done differently? If I had phoned that difficult CEO a few more times, would we have gotten the account? Would it have made any difference if we had? If I had made the coffee and washed the cups every day, would I have been too indispensable to my boss's comfort for him to let me go?"

Tyler silenced his wife with a kiss on her lips. "Don't do this, Brooke," he murmured against her cheek. "God has a purpose in all this, and as time unfolds, we'll see a blessing in the whole affair. In the meantime, you need some distraction." He leaned over to retrieve the newspaper from the floor.

"Look, here's an ad for a class on how to make a Log Cabin quilt. You've often said you wanted to learn to quilt when life settled down. Maybe it's the other way around. Learn to quilt, and then you'll settle down in life."

Brooke decided to give the quilting class a try. After all, it would be more profitable than wearing a track in her rug from pacing the floor.

Planning colors that blended together, cutting even, rectangular "logs," then sewing them one to another: She enjoyed having something constructive to think about and do. The orderliness of the process brought peace to her tormented mind.

Months later, Brooke told Tyler over dinner, "You know, I think your suggestion to learn to quilt saved my sanity. It actually calmed me down enough that I've stopped worrying about the past and started looking toward the future. I'm going to polish my résumé and find that new job!"

The Master Pattern

Peace I leave with you; my peace I give you. I do not give to you as the world gives. Do not let your hearts be troubled and do not be afraid.

John 14:27

The peace of God is available to us in every circumstance of our lives. Sometimes the hurry of life interferes with our daily communication with him, and we lose that sense of peace. He has never left us. If we simply spend time talking to God and listening to his words in our hearts, we will find that peace beyond understanding will descend upon us and overcome what troubles us.

God, flood my heart and mind with your peace. Allow me to hear your whispers of quiet calm in my life.

Cleansing Fabric, Mending Hearts

"I love the way you arranged all these pretty green and red Christmas prints," said Nora, Connie's best friend, as she picked up a completed Log Cabin square to admire it.

"I thought a Log Cabin wall hanging would make a good Christmas present for Ginger," Connie said, pointing toward the house next door.

"Do you always exchange Christmas gifts with your neighbor?" Nora asked, fingering the square.

"No, but I thought I'd better give her a present this year—to make peace, so to speak."

"Did you have a neighborly squabble?" Nora raised a questioning eyebrow.

"A squabble all right, and not very neighborly." Connie grimaced. "When we planted those azalea bushes in the side yard, we misunderstood where our property line lay and accidentally placed them on the Raymonds's land.

Ginger and her husband were as angry as if we'd planted a bed of thistles or something."

She shrugged. "Azaleas are so pretty when they bloom in the spring, we thought they would forgive us. But no. Our husbands had a big argument about digging them up and replanting them. We ended up leaving them where they were, and no one's spoken since."

Nora asked abruptly, "Connie, did you wash all your fabric before you cut out the pieces for your Christmas wall hanging?" She was examining the nearly completed quilt.

"No. What's that got to do with boundary arguments?" Connie cocked her head at her friend.

"I didn't think you had." Nora ran her hand over the sewn pieces. "Unwashed fabric feels stiff with the sizing that factories use when they manufacture material. This feels stiff."

"The stiffness makes the material easy to guide under my machine needle," Connie said, sounding defensive.

"It also means these bright red and green colors might run onto each other." Nora handed the wall hanging back to her friend. "A quilt that bleeds its color all over the place won't pacify your neighbor."

"It's too late now. All I have left to do is attach that one square, then quilt the three layers together." Connie sighed. "But you're right. If Ginger throws it in the washer and ruins it along with a load of clothes, she might get mad enough to plant thistles on our side of the line."

"Don't despair. Maybe I have a solution." Nora patted Connie's hand. "Let's wash it and see what happens. If it bleeds, I bought a soap at the grocery store that acts like a dye magnet. It sucks up the color that runs over onto the neighboring fabric."

Connie's face brightened. "Do you have a soap that sucks up the consequences of an argument with my neighbor?"

Nora only chuckled.

The dye-magnet soap took care of the reds and greens that ran when Connie washed her wall hanging. And she took care of the tension with her neighbor. When she delivered the gift, Connie apologized, and the two renewed their friendship.

The Master Pattern

This is my blood of the covenant, which is poured out for many for the forgiveness of sins.

Matthew 26:28

As we remember the amazing sacrifice of Jesus, who took the sin of the world upon himself when he went to the cross, we can summon the courage to say we are sorry and ask for forgiveness when we err. His death absorbs the stain of sin.

Lord, help me to repent quickly of my sin, and make me humble enough to ask others for their forgiveness when I offend.

Rail Fence

The Rail Fence quilt design was popular from the early days of our country. Its simple pieces enabled a quilter to use her creativity to achieve various effects, including a zigzag appearance. Some seamstresses made Rail Fence quilts as charm quilts. In a charm quilt, the crafter used fabrics only once. Girls often traded fabrics in order to gather all the hundreds of different pieces needed to complete the project. Some traditions held that the last piece in the quilt should come from a garment worn by the man the girl would marry. Because of its simplicity, the Rail Fence is still a favored pattern for children and beginners.

What a delight: to find a simple pattern that creates an exquisite result! We all long for easier maps to read, recipes to follow, instructions to heed. Life in this twenty-first century is so complicated. In this section's stories, the easy-to-make Rail Fence quilts reveal a grandma's patience and an injured young man's courage; they provide a soldier's comfort and trigger two young girls' frivolous rivalry. Can beautiful threads be found even in pain, loss, and conflict? Yes, because God is present in all of these situations. His love threads through each experience, bitter or joyous, comforting us with his constant nearness.

Quilt Day at Grandma's

"This is quilt day!" shouted nine-year-old Becca as she and her sisters waved good-bye to their mother and ran up the steps to Grandma's house.

"Grandma said I get to make a pillow first." Six-year-old Stephie preened with importance.

"Me, me." Two-year-old Katy jumped up and down as if she understood what the excitement was about.

Meeting the girls at the door with hugs, Marie asked Becca, "Did you pick out your fabrics?"

"Yes." Becca put the sack she carried on the table. "Mom tried to get me to choose something else, but I liked these best. Aren't they great?" Becca spread out a length of orange fabric, then topped it with one of purple and finally a piece of lime green.

"Bright and cheerful," Marie said, stroking her chin as she pondered the selection. "You know, I have a piece of paisley print that will blend perfectly with these and give your quilt nice unity." Marie set Becca to the task of cutting rectangular strips from her fabrics.

"While Becca cuts, you can practice on the sewing machine, Stephie."

Stephie pursed her mouth in concentration as she guided notebook paper under the needle.

When Stephie finished, Marie held the paper up to the light. "Look how nicely you followed the lines. See how it helps to practice? By the time you reached the bottom of your paper, the lines of needle holes are much straighter than the first ones."

Stephie beamed.

"After I get Becca started on sewing her pieces into a Rail Fence pattern, I'll draw some curves and a few zigzags on paper for you to practice next."

"Katy keeps stealing my pieces," Becca complained. When she pulled a fabric scrap out of Katy's fingers, the younger girl screamed.

"Now, now," Marie soothed. "There's plenty of material for everyone." She dumped some scraps from her basket on the floor near Katy. "You can arrange these so the colors look pretty together." Katy sat with her legs stretched in front of her and scattered cloth pieces far and wide.

"She's making a mess," Stephie complained.

"She's happy and out of our way," Marie corrected.

Thanks to Marie's patient instruction, her grandchildren came to enjoy sewing and creating at a young age. They began to appreciate the subtle differences in shades of colors and learned how to make pleasing combinations. They mastered the sewing machine and persevered in a project.

Most of all, they enjoyed Marie's companionship and her expectation that they would do well.

The Master Pattern

Jesus said, "Let the little children come to me, and do not hinder them, for the kingdom of heaven belongs to such as these."

Matthew 19:14

Investing time in instructing young children about quilting, but especially about God and his ways, brings lifelong benefits to their lives. Young children do not have the barriers to knowing God that can interfere when they are older. Fortunate are the children with mentors in spiritual things, who help them learn to enjoy God and expect their success in following his ways.

Make me patient with the small children in my life, so I can help form a sound spiritual foundation in their lives.

Scraps of Courage

Doug clenched his jaw, and his face reddened until he looked miserable. With every cell, he concentrated on moving his foot between the handrails he grasped.

"Good job," his nurse, Kelly, encouraged.

Doug went limp from the effort, and if it weren't for the harness holding him from the rod above, he would have fallen to the floor.

"That's enough for today," Kelly said, smiling. She rolled Doug's wheelchair up behind him. She unhooked his harness, and he fell into the chair.

"Enough? One step? What will it take to get me walking again?" Doug's face was etched with discouragement.

"This is just your first day of therapy, Mr. O'Dell. Your prognosis is excellent. I bet we'll have you walking in six months."

"That sounds like a fairy tale." Doug didn't try to make his voice pleasant.

When Madison picked her husband up in her van, she could see the lines of effort coupled with despair on her husband's face.

"One stupid second, and my whole life changed. I live it over and over," Doug said, putting his hand over his face as his wife drove home. "What did I do wrong? Why did my snowmobile fly out of control?"

"You've relived the accident enough. Let it go." Madison turned the van into their neighborhood.

"Reliving it is all I have to do. You don't know how awful it is to be stuck in that chair, my leg shattered, with no way to distract my mind from the knowledge that the man I hit died." Doug slammed his fist on the car's armrest. "Died. Dead. He isn't able to have a conversation with his wife, even a cantankerous one."

Madison was quiet. In the weeks after the accident, she had learned that whenever the conversation veered this direction, nothing she could say would help.

"Oh no. Not today!" Madison restrained a groan when she saw her friend's blue automobile at their curb.

As she steered into the driveway, several of her friends piled out of the blue car. One woman held a package while the other women helped Madison unload the wheelchair and tried to help Doug into it. He gritted his teeth and waved them away.

"Maybe it's not the best time for company," Madison whispered to her friend Molly. Doug wheeled himself into the house without so much as a grunt to acknowledge Madison's friends. "It was his first day of therapy. He's feeling down."

"That's why we made a point of coming today. Come on, follow me." Molly led the women into the house, then into the den where Doug was sitting, and placed a large package on his lap.

"Open it," the women chorused.

Doug couldn't disappoint the circle of smiling women. He opened the package. Dumbfounded, he stared and said, "You made a quilt for me?" He spread it over his lap. Fingering the rustic, woodsy-colored strips forming the Rail Fence quilt, he showed a hint of a smile.

"Look at the back." Molly flipped over a corner. Madison's quilting group had signed the quilt and written messages of hope and cheer for Doug.

At that moment, Doug lived up to his reputation as a man of few words. He couldn't say anything. He fought to keep his chin from quivering. All the phrases of thanks that popped into his mind seemed trite and inadequate for a gift representing such a large amount of time, care, and thought.

The sight of his smile was enough. Madison's own chin quivered. How she had missed her husband's engaging smile for these long months. She swallowed hard. "Thanks," she said for both of them, holding Doug's hand.

"Yeah, thanks." Doug found the moisture stinging behind his eyes mirrored in the women around him.

"We are a misty-eyed bunch," Molly said, passing the tissue box around.

Doug found his voice. "I can't believe you would go to so much trouble for me. You don't even know me very well. You see Madison at quilt guild, and I'm around only sometimes to pick her up or drop her off."

The women all talked at once. "We did it to show you our admiration for your courage."

"To let you know we care about your suffering."

"We've been praying for your recovery."

After receiving the quilt and its demonstration of love and support, Doug approached his therapy with renewed hope. Whenever he was disheartened, he put his hand on the quilt, read some of the messages on the back, and drew strength from the gift.

The Master Pattern

Carry each other's burdens, and in this way you will fulfill the law of Christ.

Galatians 6:2

Life sometimes deals us situations that are hard to take. When people rally around us, they empower us to rise up and meet our challenges. God's Word commands us to help each other when anyone is burdened.

God, make me more sensitive and responsive to people who need encouragement in difficult situations.

Don't-Cry Quilt

"Sorry I'm late," Amanda said as she bustled into the church building. "I brought more fabric." She stopped at the sight of tear-streaked faces. An awkward silence filled the room.

"Edna heard today that her son died in the war," Polly explained, continuing to stroke her friend's shoulder.

"Oh no! I'm so sorry." Amanda joined the ladies clustered around Edna.

"I decided to come quilt anyway," Edna said, raising her chin and trying to suppress the quiver of her lips. "You are my best friends, and I need you."

"Maybe we should cancel the quilting bee and go to your house. We could prepare food or something," Constance said. She picked up her basket.

"There's nothing I can do for Edward by staying home," Edna said, taking Constance's basket and setting it back down. "Mother always said busy hands are good medicine for broken hearts. Anyway, we don't know yet when we can have a decent funeral for Edward. Maybe we can have only a memorial service. He died a prisoner in Andersonville, South Carolina."

She blew her nose. "I think that's the hardest part. It wasn't a battle that took him. It was a miserable prison, a prison in the same area where my brother lives." Anger flashed across her countenance before she put her face in her hands. "Oh, my son, my son!"

"It's a terrible thing when brothers war against brothers," Polly murmured.

"Sometimes I wonder if our country can ever heal from this terrible Civil War." Constance picked up her needle again. "Maybe Edna is right. We should keep on quilting for our soldiers. So many men lie wounded in hospitals and need blankets." She began to stitch.

"I can find comfort in knowing that what we do today will warm some soldier," Edna said, wiping her eyes and settling her glasses back on her nose.

"We have enough material to finish this quilt, thanks to Amanda's weaving," Polly noted. She laid out the fabric Amanda had brought to form the backing for the Rail Fence quilt they had pieced earlier.

"It's pretty," Amanda said.

"A thrifty pattern, too." Edna tried to enter into conversation in spite of the hiccups that had replaced her sobs.

"I've used up all my scraps, even my narrow pieces, on this Rail Fence quilt," Constance said.

Slowly the level of conversation increased as the women sensed that the best way to help Edna was to continue the quilting bee.

The large group of women quilted throughout the war in their New Haven, Connecticut, church. During the Civil

War, the North and the South alike needed a large amount of bedding. Women on both sides of the war worked long hours to meet the need. There are estimates that the Northern women, by themselves, gave around a quarter of a million quilts and blankets to the war effort, probably using some forty thousand bolts of fabric. Many women made quilts without caring which army received them. The scraps of fabric that grieving and caring ladies stitched into comforters helped assuage the heartache of soldiers, no matter what the color of their uniforms.

The Master Pattern

Don't you know that you yourselves are God's temple and that God's Spirit lives in you?

1 Corinthians 3:16

People are God's creation. We become a dwelling place for God when we become Christians. Wherever we go, we find people worthy of our efforts to help and comfort them. Since all humankind is God's creation, we honor God when we help people even beyond our church family.

God, make me an instrument of aid to all of your people.

Speedy Sewing Is Sloppy Sewing

"I can rip faster than you!" Morgan shouted as she pulled the piece of fabric between her hands with a satisfying rip.

"Can not," Allie responded, tearing her own fabric. She wouldn't accept second best.

"The purpose of tearing the fabric is to ensure that our pieces for the Rail Fence quilt line up with the straight of the goods. When the pieces follow the woven line of the material weaving, we call that the straight of the goods." Mrs. Frank tried to sidetrack the rivalry she observed in her class of eight-year-old girls learning to make Rail Fence quilts. "Following that line at the edge of our pieces helps a quilt lie flat and keep its shape."

Mrs. Frank put her hand on a child's shoulder. "Not so fast, Allie. You aren't in a race."

"Morgan is." Allie pointed to the next table, where Morgan bit her lip as she maneuvered fabric pieces under the sewing machine needle.

"Slow down, girls. We aren't putting out a fire. We're learning skills."

As the day wore on, Mrs. Frank felt that the competition between Morgan and Allie was hindering the other girls' learning.

"Girls, it's more important to obtain good results than it is to finish first," she said. She held Morgan's machine-stitched pieces close to the light. "If you don't make straight seams, eventually your Rail Fence will pull and wrinkle."

"I'm going to be the first to finish," Morgan said, undeterred.

"Don't count on it." Allie pressed harder on the foot control of her machine.

Mrs. Frank's patience snapped. "Neither of you girls will be first. In fact, I daresay you may be last. Look at how your pieces pucker! Both of you take your seam rippers and pick out the last rows of stitching you have made. Then start over. You must sew these pieces evenly."

Ignoring the sullen glares of both girls, Mrs. Frank handed them seam rippers and unplugged their sewing machines. The other girls giggled.

The Master Pattern

We do not dare to classify or compare ourselves with some who commend themselves. When they measure themselves by themselves and compare themselves with themselves, they are not wise.

2 Corinthians 10:12

Morgan and Allie placed competition with one another ahead of completing a satisfactory quilt. Even adults must resist the temptation to compare their talents and accomplishments with those of others. If we are wise, we will concentrate on doing our best with each task, pursuing excellence. If we are wise, we will resist allowing ourselves to feel jealous of others' skills. Instead, we will rejoice about their success.

God, I want to feel glad when other people use their abilities to accomplish and succeed. Help me not to compare myself with others, but instead to strive to achieve your goals for my life.

Threading Hope into Despair

"Not again!" Robin ran to her son when she saw him stiffen. She wasn't in time to ease his fall, but she quickly checked to see if his airway was open. She reached for the quilt on the sofa and put it under his head and thrashing limbs, resisting the temptation to avert her eyes so as not to see how the miserable seizure distorted his face and body.

After minutes that felt like hours to Robin's frantic mind, Danny's nine-year-old body finally relaxed. Sobbing, he rolled into her embrace. "There, there," Robin crooned over and over as their tears mingled. Meaningless words were all she could think to say.

"Why do I keep having these seizures?" Danny asked. "What's wrong with me?" He clung to his mother as if by doing so, he could hide from the devastating attacks.

Robin smoothed his hair and patted his back. "The doctors are trying to find out. All they know is that the brain is involved somehow. Your case has baffled them." A sense of helplessness overwhelmed her.

"Can't they give me the right medicine? I'd take a shot if it'd help," Danny pleaded. "Tryouts for the Little League team are next week. I want to play ball." He pounded his fist on his thigh and sobbed anew.

Robin slid backward on the floor, holding her son until their backs rested against the front of the sofa.

Over the next months, the scene repeated itself again and again, until Robin felt as if she were caught in a concrete mixer and couldn't climb out. Her world tumbled in dizzy circles with each seizure, and the doctors' inability to diagnose or treat Danny lingered. Despair engulfed her.

The local children's hospital assembled an excellent medical team, but before it could provide answers or help, an especially violent seizure threw Danny into a coma. He never woke up.

"I'm so sorry."

"What a terrible loss."

"How painful, to lose a child so young."

Robin nodded and stared blankly as people rallied around her, trying to help. She couldn't think of anything to say. All the offers of sympathy seemed no more useful than the pointless "There, there" she used to murmur over Danny.

In her agony, Robin grew fearful. "I think I'm losing my mind," she told her son's doctor when he called to check on her.

He responded in a kind voice, "The women at the children's hospital are making quilts as a fund-raiser for research into problems like Danny's. A class is being held Saturday. The participants will learn how to make a Rail Fence quilt in a day." The doctor cleared his throat. "If you can take part, the funds may help some other boy like Danny."

For the first time since Danny's death, Robin felt something penetrate her mind-numbing fog and prick her interest.

A few days later, Robin and the other women were selecting fabrics. "Look how pretty this blue looks against the blue and green paisley print," she remarked. Soon the others in the class recognized Robin's sharp color instincts, and they asked her what fabrics to combine and how to arrange the rails from dark to light.

At night, Robin's dreams haunted her with replays of her efforts to keep Danny from harming himself during an attack. By day, she found that her quilting blocked out the painful visions of Danny twisted by seizures.

"I think quilting helps me heal," Robin told her quilting group. "When I focus on the beauty of the fabric, the intricacy of the design, I can stop focusing on the mental pictures of Danny's suffering. I can keep from dwelling on my loss when I concentrate on creating a beautiful quilt."

The Master Pattern

The LORD has anointed me . . .
   [to] provide for those who grieve in Zion—
to bestow on them a crown of beauty
   instead of ashes,
the oil of gladness
   instead of mourning,
and a garment of praise
   instead of a spirit of despair.

They will be called oaks of righteousness,
a planting of the LORD
for the display of his splendor.

Isaiah 61:1, 3

Whatever the source of grief and pain in our lives, God will provide a way out of the despair when we ask him. He will take our ashes of disappointment, our mourning for broken dreams, and our desperation over heartaches and exchange them all for gladness in our God. He will help us substitute instead a spirit of praise to our Savior and discover new depths of his splendor.

God, help us turn our sorrows over to you for your transformation.

Flying Geese

Flying Geese quilts vary widely in the arrangement of
the triangles, which represent birds in flight. The pioneer
woman was close to nature, so the common sight of geese
migrating probably inspired the name for this quilt. Because
patterns did not appear in printed magazines and catalogs
before the nineteenth century, seamstresses shared these
groupings of triangular pieces among themselves. Quilts
dating back to 1785 have carried the flying geese motif. The

simplicity of the triangle design made this an easy pattern to copy, and it enjoyed great popularity.

Flying geese? Corn husks? Cotton seeds? Mystery novels? Quilt rulers? Yes, these familiar objects set the scenes in stories about hospitality, inaccurate measuring (of people, not fabric), and families that work together. In each, beautiful threads form the tie that binds hearts together in lasting ways.

Measure Up

Nancy slid her ticket stub into the box for the door prize and followed her friends into the quilt symposium. "Wow, this is going to be fun," she said as she looked around the huge room. "I've never seen so many quilts in one place."

"I knew you'd like it, even if you aren't a guild member or even a quilter," Cheryl said, smiling.

"I'm astonished." Nancy stood in front of a quilt made of tiny pieces of fabric arranged in a careful progression of shades. The overall effect was of a girl's face sniffing a flower in a garden. "It's almost as if a person painted a picture but used fabric instead of paint."

"Exactly," answered Dorie, who stood with the group of friends admiring the prize-winning quilt.

"But look at all those itsy-bitsy pieces. I can't imagine the patience or artistry required to create this. What a masterpiece!" Nancy shook her head. "If you thought you'd get me interested in quilting, you thought wrong. These intricate pictures intimidate me."

"Let's go to another display of quilts made from more common patterns," Cheryl said and led the way.

As she walked through the display, Nancy commented, "You may call these Flying Geese quilts simple, but I think they look hard to do."

"Having the right equipment helps. Some of the rulers are expensive, so I have to accumulate them a few at a time," Dorie said.

With a squawk, the loudspeaker came on. "Have your ticket ready, and check the upper-right-hand corner as I read the number for the first door-prize winner for the morning."

Nancy almost didn't bother to pull her ticket from her pocket, but Cheryl nudged her. "I won!" Nancy shouted in disbelief.

"Let's go see what you won." The friends trooped over to the entrance together.

"Here you go." The woman on duty handed over a large box filled with rulers of every size, shape, and kind, suitable for a multitude of quilting tasks.

"Hey, no fair! What a great prize, and you aren't even a member of a quilt guild!" Dorie said.

Because Dorie smiled, Nancy knew she was joking.

"Guess now's the time to start. I haven't the faintest idea what to do with these things." Nancy shook the box. "But I'm going to learn. Where was that class sign-up sheet we passed?"

Nancy's friends considered the prize wasted on her, but the rulers started her on an unexpectedly satisfying hobby. One Flying Geese quilt later, Nancy was hooked.

The Master Pattern

But the LORD said to Samuel, "Do not consider his appearance or his height, for I have rejected him. The LORD does not look at the things man looks at. Man looks at the outward appearance, but the LORD looks at the heart."

1 Samuel 16:7

Nancy's friends thought her lack of skills made her unworthy to win the prize. God's method of measuring people is different from the world's. When Samuel set out to anoint a king, the Lord told him not to look on appearance. We are wise to heed this advice in our relationships. We need to expend time and effort to discover what lies within a person's heart, but our evaluations are more accurate if we search for what God has planted in him or her.

I want to see the inner hearts of the people around me.
Keep me from evaluating people by superficial standards.

Creating Quilts, Finding Friends

Tammy let the quilt square drop to the floor and her head flop back on her pillow. "I don't have the strength to quilt since chemotherapy started. This nasty cancer not only threatens my life, it's stealing my hobby." She raised a fist, only to let it drop helplessly on her mattress.

"Only temporarily." Her husband, Blake, picked up the discarded material and tucked it in a basket by the bed. "Our hope is that the chemo is giving you more years to do lots more quilting. Do you feel well enough to read?" Blake laid a book beside her.

"*Goose on a Pond*?" Tammy read the title and the blurb on the back cover. "A mystery about a quilt. Sounds like it should keep me distracted from my treatments."

"That's my hope." Blake hugged his wife.

Blake kept Tammy supplied with one after another of the books from the compelling quilt-mystery series. Each book, with a title reflecting the name of a quilt pattern, buoyed Tammy's spirits while she completed her treatment. Grateful for the good reading that helped her endure miserable therapy, she e-mailed the author, who graciously replied. By the time Tammy recovered, the continuing e-mails had established a friendship.

As soon as she felt better, Tammy asked Blake to take her to the quilt shop. "I think I'm ready to begin quilting again, and I'd like to make one for my favorite author."

Blake offered advice about the designs for the quilt squares, one for each pattern used in the book titles. Tammy began with the Flying Geese. She stitched her love and appreciation into the quilt and mailed it off.

Months later, Tammy's squeal brought Blake running. Tammy held a letter in her hand. Touched by the quilt gift, the author had invited the couple to visit her.

A year passed. One day, Tammy waved a book in Blake's face. "Guess what?"

"What?" Blake leaned back to look at the novel's cover.

"We are characters in this book."

"Really?"

Sure enough, the author had developed two of her minor book characters based on the couple. Their flourishing friendship provided one of Tammy's silver linings from her illness.

The Master Pattern

A man that hath friends must shew himself friendly: and there is a friend that sticketh closer than a brother.

Proverbs 18:24 KJV

In an ancient child's story, a goose states a wise truth: "One can never have too many friends." A loyal chum brings joy, comfort, and fun to life. Making overtures to establish a friendship is always worth the effort. How amazing that God, the Creator of the universe, wants to be our friend, and he took the first step toward us.

Thank you, God, for being my friend. Show me how to hone my friendship skills.

Cold Nights and Corn Husks

"Timothy, are you taking a nap under there?" Clara leaned over in her chair and peeked under the quilt frame. Six-year-old Timothy sat cross-legged, forming letters with the snips of thread lying on the floor.

"I'm practicing my alphabet." He couldn't suppress a giggle at his excuse, and his mother laughed with him.

"Well, Mr. Shakespeare-in-the-making, there are cold nights between now and your literary success, so keep your mind on your quilt job. Unless you poke this needle back to me the minute I stick it through these tough corn husks, it will be Christmas before I finish this quilt."

"Why do we have to use corn husks in our quilts? Our old blankets were softer, and I didn't have to sit under here forever to poke up needles."

"Don't whine, Timothy. We don't have any more old blanket pieces to use in the middle of our quilts." Clara punched her needle through the top of the quilt, then Timothy took it and stuck it back up toward his mother.

She pulled the thread through and repeated the process. "Be glad we have corn husks."

"They rattle when I sleep and wake me up." Timothy put his hand over his head and jiggled the quilt to demonstrate.

"True enough, but they provide warmth. Fabric is scarce in the colonies." Clara and Timothy now had a fast rhythm going, passing the needle back and forth through the three layers of the quilt. "Your father hopes to have saved enough to buy some sheep by the time 1735 turns into 1736. Then we can card wool for softer quilts."

"Do I have to card the wool, too?"

"Probably. It takes us all to get the work done. I couldn't sew this fast without your passing the needle up to me. It's impossible to make a complete stitch myself through a layer of stiff husks."

Under the cover of the quilt frame, Timothy protested, "It's Deborah's turn."

"Her turn comes after she cuts the triangles for the next Flying Geese quilt."

"Why does she make so many little triangles?"

"Because tiny pieces that aren't useful for anything else make fine flying geese in a quilt. When you sew enough small pieces together, you have a warm, comforting blanket." Clara reached under the quilt to tickle Timothy under his arm. "If your wiggly little body stays still long enough to keep under a cover, that is."

Deborah turned to see what was funny. "What am I missing?"

"Needle poking." Timothy crawled out from under the quilt. "Here, it's your turn."

"Do I have to?" Deborah groaned. "At church, Missy says her mother imports blankets from England. I'm going to ask her mother if that's true. I think Missy just wants us to think she's better than everybody."

"Mind your own business. Working with your hands is honorable." Clara lifted up the quilt and motioned for Deborah to crawl underneath the frame.

The Master Pattern

Make it your ambition to lead a quiet life, to mind your own business and to work with your hands, just as we told you.

1 Thessalonians 4:11

Work is a blessing from God. Even uncompensated work benefits us, because a job well done brings us satisfaction and a sense of worth. When we stay busy with fruitful activity, we don't have time or as much inclination to busy ourselves with other people's business. Just as Deborah did not need to fuel her suspicions that Missy was untruthful about owning valuable blankets, wisdom steers us not to probe into other people's lives merely to satisfy our curiosity. When we occupy our hands and minds with productive work, we contribute to our well-being.

Thank you, God, for opportunities to work. Help me to discern the difference between genuine interest in friends and interfering where I am not wanted or needed.

Bumpy Bedding

"Did you see Helen's Flying Geese quilt?" Eveline whispered to her friend behind her hand. She was arranging food for the church picnic on a table of board planks. Families had spread quilts on the lawn for seating.

"No, why?" Hester asked.

"It's full of cotton seeds," Eveline answered. "Our family had to spend several nights with Helen's family after a fire destroyed some of our roof. All the quilts on their beds have lumps. The Calhouns used cotton with the seeds still attached."

Hester looked puzzled. "Why don't the Calhouns get their slaves to pick the seeds out of the cotton the way we do?"

"Maybe they don't have enough slaves. I saw only one in the kitchen and one in the barn while we were there."

"Jared said next cotton season, we won't use our slaves to pick the seeds out. There's a new machine called a cotton gin, and it takes the seeds out. Pretty soon there will be a machine close enough that we can take our cotton to it for processing." Hester's eyes sparkled. "I think Jared has some idea he'd like to free our slaves. He said Eli Whitney would go down in history as a great man because he invented such an important machine."

"You'd know how important if you ever slept on a Calhoun quilt."

"Hush, Eveline. You shouldn't say bad things about the people who offered you hospitality when you had a fire." Hester tugged at Eveline's sleeve. "Shhh, here comes Helen now. You don't want her to hear you criticizing her quilts."

"Hello, Hester, Eveline," Helen greeted the women. "I've missed seeing you since your roof was fixed, Eveline. I enjoyed our time together before you moved back home."

"We've been busy getting the house back in order since the fire," Eveline explained.

"Maybe we can see more of each other at Christmas. A whole lot of cousins are coming to visit for the holidays, and we'll need to put some of them up in neighbors' homes. We wondered if your family would keep some of them." Helen looked expectantly at Eveline.

"Extra people at Christmastime would be inconvenient. I don't see how we could manage additional people. Why, I'm not sure we would even have enough bedding for company."

"Oh." Helen's smile froze on her face. "Of course, if it's too much trouble . . ."

"I can help," Hester said before Helen could finish. Hoping to distract Helen from Eveline's thoughtless answer,

Hester began to talk about where people could sleep and what pretty quilts she'd set out for them.

"We're going to take our cotton to the new cotton gin at harvest. It removes the seeds," Eveline interrupted.

Hester wanted to clap a hand over Eveline's mouth. Instead, she grabbed Eveline's arm and began to back away. "I forgot that we said we'd cut the pies for dessert."

"Eveline, where is your hospitality?" Hester practically hissed through clenched teeth as she dragged her friend into the church door.

The Master Pattern

You blind guides! You strain out a gnat but swallow a camel.

Matthew 23:24

Why do you look at the speck of sawdust in your brother's eye and pay no attention to the plank in your own eye? How can you say to your brother, "Let me take the speck out of your eye," when all the time there is a plank in your own eye? You hypocrite, first take the plank out of your own eye, and then you will see clearly to remove the speck from your brother's eye.

Matthew 7:3–5

Finding fault with others is easy. Recognizing and admitting our own failures is a different matter. Often we are reluctant to see ourselves truthfully. The temptation is to focus on whatever small flaws we find offensive in another while we ignore larger ones in ourselves. This is what

Eveline did when she belittled Helen's quilts yet didn't recognize her own lack of hospitality. God's forgiveness is big enough for all our errors, big or small. A humble person tries to overlook other people's foibles, knowing she often needs forgiving grace herself.

Lord, grant me the humility to recognize my failings and to ask for your help with them. Give me the grace not to notice the defects of others but to extend them mercy as you extend it to me.

Double Wedding
Ring

Before 1825, the Double Wedding Ring pattern was known by more than forty names, including Endless Chain and Around the World. It grew in popularity during the late 1920s, when women cut the curved pieces for the rings from patterns made from the sturdy pages of Sears Roebuck and Montgomery Ward catalogs. The number of pieces in a ring varied from four to twelve; older quilts tended to consist of wider bands for the rings. In the days when some communities admonished young women to prepare at least a dozen quilts before she married, the Double Wedding Ring was often the last one added to her hope chest. Friends and family frequently held a quilting bee to finish it before the wedding.

A wedding is always a joyous event, and our lives are filled with such celebrations. Yet we know that along with beautiful threads run more sinister ones: illness, cruelty, homesickness. In these stories, and in our daily lives, we see that we can choose which threads will inform our reactions, create our attitudes, and decide our actions. Beauty is there for the taking—and making.

High Value, Low Price

The sight of several quilts spread over long tables in a neighborhood yard sale prompted Cathy to pull her car over to the curb. "How much are the quilts?" she asked the woman by a cash box.

"Oh, I hadn't thought about a price. I put them out to cover the tables and make our sale look attractive. They're old. I guess three dollars would be about right."

"Three dollars each?" Cathy couldn't believe she heard correctly.

"Yes, but if you want them, you'll have to move all the stuff on top of them. I've lifted and stooped enough for one day, getting this stuff marked and ready for the garage sale."

"I'll be glad to do that. Where do you want me to put the items while I move the quilts?" Cathy tried not to sound too excited. She didn't want to drive up the price.

"Anywhere will be fine. Just make sure everything's back on the table when you're through."

Cathy started at one end of the table and moved the dishes, vases, and pans to the grass under the table, where

she wouldn't step on them. She leaned over to look carefully at the Double Wedding Ring quilt she uncovered.
Someone with talent had made the tiny stitches. The pastel
colors were perfect for her guest room. She hurried when
she saw another car pull up to the curb. She wanted to buy
the other two quilts also.

She folded the quilt with the pattern to the inside so as
not to attract attention to the fact one could buy the table
covers. "Here," she told the bored-looking cash-box lady.
"Hold this for me while I get another one." She hastily
piled the glassware back on the table and moved on to
the next table. The people from the car were looking at
the toys on the lawn.

Good, that gives me more time, she thought. She glanced
around for a clean place where she could pile the baby
clothes spread out on the table. She stacked the clothes on
a nearby lawn chair and took a good look at the quilt. She
was delighted with its single-ring design. She recognized
it as the Friendship Knot version of the Double Wedding
Ring quilt. By the time she reached the last table and folded
up the variation called Pickle Dish, she could hardly believe her good fortune. She'd found three variations of the
Double Wedding Ring pattern in the same sale.

With her quilts safely purchased and deposited in her
car, Cathy looked around at the other items for sale. "My
granddaughter loves horses," she said to another lady looking at some paintings of running horses. "What a good
birthday present for Jill."

She selected one and looked closer while she waited at
the cash box for the home owner to finish with the person in
front of her. *Remington.* She looked wide-eyed at the famous

signature. "Paintings by Remington for fifteen dollars?" she muttered and turned back to pick out another one.

The home owner finished with her customer and called to Cathy, "Are you ready?" She chatted as Cathy came over. "Won't my husband be surprised when he comes home from his business trip? John's been wanting to clean out the garage for a year." The gray-headed lady put the money from the previous sale in her box and began straightening the bills and change.

With a Remington picture in each hand, Cathy said, "I'm sure your husband will think you've done a thorough job." Juggling the pictures, she was struggling to open her purse when a man in a suit ran up the driveway, his tie flapping over his shoulder.

"Eleanor, what are you doing?" The man snatched the painting out of Cathy's hand.

"You're back early." Eleanor continued to tidy up the cash box. "I'm surprising you by cleaning out the garage. I figured a yard sale was the best way to get rid of the junk." She beamed at the man.

"Junk! These are my Remington paintings!" He waved his arm to include the other one Cathy held and the ones still leaning against the lawn chairs. "You're selling price-less paintings for fifteen dollars apiece!" He banged his fist on the card table holding the cash box. Some of the coins bounced so high they landed outside of the box.

Cathy hoped the man's bright red face did not foretell a stroke right there in his driveway.

"Well, I haven't sold any yet." She gestured toward Cathy. "This lady is the first to want one, and she hasn't paid for it."

Silently, Cathy handed the angry man the other painting she held.

"John, how was I to guess you wanted to keep them?" The lady's face was beginning to match her gray hair. "They weren't hung up or anything. They were just stashed in a box."

"The box I packed when I cleaned out my dad's house. I'll get around to hanging them." The man's coloring looked less dangerous now.

"Would you like the quilts back?" Cathy gestured toward her car, where she had left them. "They're worth more than I paid."

John ran his hand through his hair and turned to his wife. "Did you sell your grandmother's inheritance, too? Isn't anything around here priceless?"

"You are." Eleanor put her arms around her husband.

"You mean I'm not for sale?" John returned the hug and the tension drained from the couple.

"You're a gift from God without price."

Eleanor told Cathy to keep the quilts. And every time Cathy saw them she remembered God's gifts are both free and priceless.

The Master Pattern

Peter answered: "May your money perish with you, because you thought you could buy the gift of God with money!"

Acts 8:20

In Acts 8, a man named Simon had seen the power of the Holy Spirit and wanted to purchase it. The benefits of the Holy Spirit are not for sale. They are gifts from God that he delights to give his people. Salvation is also free: No one can buy it at any price. Valuable paintings or irreplaceable heirlooms are insignificant when we compare them with the priceless spiritual gifts God gives those who follow him.

Thank you, Lord, for your gift of salvation and for your provision of the Holy Spirit. I want to keep knowing you as my first priority. I want to give you the highest value in my life.

Red Thread for a Blue Day

"Victoria, settle down." Margaret picked up the pile of *McCall's* magazines her restless granddaughter had spilled from the nearby table.

"I'm sorry." Victoria fidgeted with a doily on the table, then walked to the window overlooking Margaret's garden. "I'm tired of staying inside. I wanted to feed the fish in your little pond and make dolls out of hollyhock flowers, but all it does is rain, rain, rain."

Margaret joined her at the window. "I'm getting tired of gray skies myself."

"Gray. It's all gray since my sister had to go to the hospital. We don't do anything fun anymore, and I have to spend the whole summer here instead of home." Victoria's voice trembled. "I miss Mama."

Margaret gathered her granddaughter in a long hug. Victoria's tears dampened the front of Margaret's blouse. "Sometimes tears are good. It's as if they wash away our grief," Margaret said, patting Victoria's back. "You know how pretty the world looks after a good rain? With all the

170

dust and pollen washed away, all the plants and leaves are shiny. Crying can heal our souls when we're sad."

They stood together for a while, arms around each other, watching the rain pouring through the branches of the oak tree and bouncing off the stones around the fish pond.

After a time, Margaret began sorting through a stack of weekly newspapers. "Look here, Victoria." Margaret showed her an advertisement for an embroidery pattern in the paper.

Victoria looked at the red cardinal in the picture. "That's the Virginia state bird."

"You're right. I've been buying patterns for the state birds. The newspaper advertises a different one each week. Would you like to embroider these while you visit this summer?"

"Do you think I'm big enough?"

"Of course. Haven't you made your sampler? Modern 1930s girls around here all make samplers to practice their needlework."

"Yes, but birds would be more fun to embroider than the alphabet and numbers." Victoria ran her finger over the bird pictured in the newspaper.

Margaret said, "I've finished piecing a Double Wedding Ring quilt for your mother and father's anniversary gift. It would look beautiful with an embroidered bird in the center of each ring. Your needlework would add an extra-special touch." She took several packets of patterns from a drawer and spread them out. "Would you like to do that?"

"Can I do the cardinal first? Do you have red embroidery floss to make his outline?"

Victoria did a fine job embroidering the bird and selected Maryland's state bird, the Baltimore oriole, for the next ring.

Noting her granddaughter's happy face, Margaret commented, "The handwork cheered you up, didn't it? I'm pleased that God provided a way to make you feel better. He will do the same for your sister as she heals in the hospital. He has good plans for all of us."

The Master Pattern

My soul, wait thou only upon God; for my expectation is from him.

Psalm 62:5 KJV

"For I know the plans I have for you," declares the LORD, "plans to prosper you and not to harm you, plans to give you hope and a future."

Jeremiah 29:11

When problems pile up in our lives, these are good verses to remember. God wants blessings for us. He can supply hope where there is no hope. He can create a future when it appears we have only damaged dreams. Out of the difficulties that rain on our lives, God's plan can grow.

Thank you for the good plans you have for my life. Help me to recognize and cooperate with them.

Things That Prick:
Needles—and Words

"Would you please hold these quilt needles and thimbles for us?" Cameron asked the clerk as she laid a little pile of quilt supplies beside the cash register. "We're going upstairs to look at the quilts before we make our purchases."

Wendy put several bolts of fabric on the counter next to the supplies. "If we find a quilt already made out of matching colors for my bedroom, maybe I won't buy this material to make my own."

As they climbed the stairs to the quilt display, Cameron said, "I don't know when I've enjoyed an afternoon so much."

"A fancy lunch and beautiful quilts: the perfect day," Wendy agreed.

"This is some store." Cameron stopped at the top of the stairs. "I don't think I've ever seen so many quilts for sale in one place."

"Hanging them on swinging rods makes room for lots of them, and we can still see the whole quilt by swinging the others out of the way."

The women began to swing the quilts, one by one, from right to left to get a good view of each. They were careful to handle only the long piece of muslin carefully basted for protection to the outer edge of each quilt.

When they reached a group of Double Wedding Ring quilts, Wendy exclaimed, "That's the pattern I want!"

"I hear the curves of the rings makes this pattern a hard one."

"That's what my teacher said. Maybe I'll buy one of these beauties and stick to simpler patterns when I make a quilt." Forgetting to handle only the muslin protector, Wendy stepped forward and ran her hand over the quilt. "Which one is prettiest for my bedroom?"

"A hard choice." Cameron tried to tug one into more direct light. "Is this color more pink or peach?"

"Peach wouldn't be as good with my drapes. How about one where blue shades are more dominant?" Wendy stepped between the quilts to examine the blue more closely, then turned to her friend, saying, "Buying a Double Wedding Ring quilt will make this an even more perfect day."

"And just what do you think you're doing?"

Wendy jumped at the voice shouting from the other side of the room. She looked up to see who was yelling and why.

"Is that man talking to us?" Cameron whispered.

"He's bearing down on us like a wounded bear with rabies."

"He's angry, all right."

The man waved his arms. "Get your hands off my quilts."

Everyone in the store stood still.

Wendy slid out from between the quilts, and Cameron put her hands down at her sides. Then she took a step back as the large man loomed in front of the two ladies. With an angry swing of his arm, he repositioned the quilts to hang in straight, parallel rows.

"Do not touch." He pointed to a sign posted on the wall high above the quilts. "Are you both illiterate?"

Wendy leaned her head way back to see the sign. "I'm sorry." Her voice had more squeak than volume. She cleared her throat and tried again. "I was so excited about the quilts, I forgot."

She stared at the veins standing out on the man's neck. "I was deciding which quilt to buy."

"You need to buy several after manhandling them."

"I'm really very sorry," Wendy said. She grabbed Cameron's hand, pulled her down the steps, and practically slunk out the door of the store.

"We wouldn't buy one of your precious quilts if they were the last ones on earth!" Cameron sputtered. "You sure were self-controlled," she told Wendy. "I wanted to yell back at him as loud as he yelled at us."

"It wasn't self-control. I was so scared that my voice box froze."

"How does the man stay in business, with such poor public relations? He told us off in front of the entire store."

The Master Pattern

The tongue of the righteous is choice silver,
but the heart of the wicked is of little value.

Proverbs 10:20

The proprietor of the quilt store lost Wendy's business because he spoke harshly to her. When you face angry people, ask God to help you respond with grace. The ability to speak with a gracious tongue is as valuable as silver and can mollify anger.

God, give me a tongue of silver when I speak to others.

Few Minutes, Many Stitches

Gladys secured her needle in the material and put the quilt down on her lap. She shifted into first gear, then eased her small pickup forward the length of one more tanker truck in the long line of waiting milk trucks. She leaned out the window to estimate how much longer before she could unload her cans at the milk-receiving plant. Not more than another hour before she could sell her farm's milk and head for home, she decided.

"Every day when I look at those enormous trucks, I have to laugh." Gladys scratched the ears of her French poodle on the seat beside her. "My little red pickup looks as ridiculous sandwiched between these monster trucks as you do when I walk you and Buster together. That Great Dane could snap a toy poodle like you in two if he wanted."

Gigi wagged her tail as if in agreement.

"When I first started bringing the milk here, I worried some trucker wouldn't see me and would back up into my truck and smash it flat," Gladys said as she picked up her quilt again. She began to appliqué more wedges in her Double Wedding Ring pattern.

"Auntie Gladys." Two brown eyes peeped into the car window.

Gladys reached over and unlatched the door. "Climb in, Libby. I wondered if you were going to come visit Gigi and me today." Gladys picked up Gigi, who was turning in circles on the front seat. She closed her hand over the dog's yipping mouth. "Someday Gigi will wiggle herself in half. She gets so excited to see you."

Gigi settled on Libby's lap, and Gladys returned to her quilt making.

"Why do you always quilt in your truck?" Libby asked.

"Because the good Lord gave me the time to fill, and I don't want to waste it. Minutes add up to hours, and it's surprising how much one can accomplish by using every minute—even those spent waiting."

"I can't come tomorrow. You and Gigi will have to wait in line by yourselves. I have to go to the hospital for my breathing treatment. I hate it!" Libby's frown was replaced by a giggle when Gigi licked her face.

"Remember what we talked about yesterday, and you'll get through the treatment." Gladys patted Libby's hand.

"I remember. 'Let everything that has breath praise the Lord.' I'll let my insides praise the Lord, even if I can't talk with that nasty thing in my mouth."

"Thatta girl."

Gladys handed Libby the quilt to hold while she put the truck in gear and moved forward another truck length.

After chatting some more, Libby hopped out to return to her home next to the road.

Gladys stitched and prayed for Libby and her family.

The Master Pattern

Be wise in the way you act toward outsiders; make the most of every opportunity.

Colossians 4:5

Although Gladys endured long waits every day to sell her milk, she learned to put the time to good use. Time is too precious to waste. Whether we spend it accomplishing work, pursuing a hobby, or simply refreshing ourselves with recreation, we should ask God how best to employ his gift of time. One idea: Discussing God's goodness and praying for others is time well spent.

God, show me how you want me to use my time. Remind me to take advantage of every small chunk of it.

Baltimore Album

The spectacular Baltimore Album quilts originated in Baltimore, Maryland, at a time when production of cotton cloth was the city's largest industry. The elaborate quilts were more popular where life allowed ladies some ease to do intricate needlework and the funds to use fine cloth, sometimes imported. The use of appliqué permitted the quilter to depict any kind of flower, animal, or scene she desired. Sometimes these were called Friendship quilts:

One person purchased the fabric and distributed it to different people, who each created one square for the project. The coordinator threw a party to gather the squares together. Then the women enjoyed a quilting bee to finish the coverlet. The custom of signing the block a person made and including poetry or Scripture verses added to the interest of the quilts.

Here the beautiful threads of a Baltimore Album quilt create stories of reverence for a reverend, restoration for tattered pieces, a pitchfork in the right place at the right time, and prayers said over a Peruvian quilt. These characters learn how to honor a faithful servant, where puppies belong, how God's power can overwhelm life-threatening pest bites, and why three holes in a favorite quilt are a good thing. In all, a master pattern is at work, and the Craftsman shows the way.

The Gift of Stitches

"Thank you for coming," Christy said when she answered her doorbell. After helping her friend Delia with her coat, she motioned her toward the living room, where a number of women from their church had already gathered.

"Help yourself to some sandwiches and cookies from the sideboard. Lucille will pour tea. When everyone is served, we'll discuss our plans for Pastor Greene's Baltimore Album quilt."

Christy was in charge of the celebration for the beloved man. "I want an extra-special quilt for him," she said. "In January 1875, he will have served our Baltimore church for fifteen years. Remember, it's all hush-hush." Christy put her finger to her lips. "We want the gift to be a surprise."

How on earth will so many different personalities manage to agree on one quilt? she wondered, watching the women fill their plates.

"Here, Ruby, you missed the best pimento-cheese sandwiches," Christy said, piling two more sandwiches on Ruby's plate in spite of her protests. Ruby was more agreeable when well fed.

"Wouldn't you prefer lemonade?" Christy held out a glass to Faye before she reached Lucille and the teapot. Tea made a chatterbox out of Faye, and Christy hoped to allow the more timid women an opportunity to give their ideas.

"I'll contribute the red material so all the squares will be the same shade," Virginia offered.

"I'll bring the green," Delia chimed in.

"Why do Baltimore Album quilts always display so much red and green?" Faye complained. "I think we should include lots of other colors."

Christy jumped in to stave off an argument, saying, "We can. I'll bring blue. I like blue for a cross on at least one square, and we need someone to include a church somewhere."

"Maybe a harp, too, because Pastor Greene is so fond of our worship music," Candace added, as she mimicked plucking a harp. "I'll bring yellow for the harp and all the flower centers."

"I want purple centers in my flower basket," Ruby countered. "Of course, I'll make a square with a basket of flowers. I make the most intricate, elegant pattern."

"What's a simple pattern I could sew? All those swirls and leaves make me a nervous wreck," Candace said, shuddering.

"How about sewing the border? Perhaps a simple band of alternating red and white triangles would set off the elaborate squares," Faye suggested.

184

Much to Christy's relief, the afternoon ended with a workable plan. Each woman was to bring a particular fabric and to create the pattern for her square.

"I'll have the next meeting at my house," Candace volunteered. "We'll all bring our materials and cut the pieces together, so we are using the same fabrics."

"A unified effect," Ruby agreed.

Not long into the next meeting, Candace was almost sorry she had offered her house. By the time all the women had cut their leaves from the green and their flowers, berries, and ribbons from the red, the rug looked like a garden: bits of colored material and threads scattered everywhere. "Don't worry," Candace told Elsie, who was working in the kitchen. "I'll see you're paid extra for cleaning up our mess."

"I'll host the arranging party," Faye said as the women gathered their pieces to take home and appliqué. "We can lay the squares out on my hall floor, then stand on my circular stairs for a good perspective on which arrangement gives the best balance to the piece. How long will we need to make our squares at home before we meet again?"

At the meeting in Faye's house, Christy told Callie, "I'm so glad you could come this time. We need someone to draw all the fine details on the squares as well as ink Pastor Greene's name and celebration date in the square with the cross. Since you're so good with pen and ink, would you do those touches today?"

After Callie agreed, Christy sewed the squares together and basted the top to the back, ready for the quilting bee. "I hope Pastor likes it," she said.

"He'll know we consider his labor among us worthy of reward," Callie assured her.

"I'm going to be sorry when our quilt is done, and we don't have the reason to get together anymore," Ruby said as the quilting progressed.

"If Christy's daughter marries her Baltimore sailor, we can do it all over again for a wedding gift," Candace said.

"Except we must appliqué ships on it," Faye added.

"And put in more blue to represent the sea," Ruby offered.

"I'll buy the green again," Candace volunteered.

"We won't have the excuse for a planning meeting if we keep this up," Ruby warned.

Pleasant conversation accompanied by large quantities of laughter ensured that the women would continue to quilt together and enjoy one another's company for a long time to come.

The Master Pattern

For the Scripture says, "Do not muzzle the ox while it is treading out the grain," and "The worker deserves his wages."

1 Timothy 5:18

Making a quilt to honor a minister was common in the nineteenth century. Ministers worked hard, and sometimes their congregations had difficulty scraping together enough money to pay the men decent salaries. Even today, a pastor's life requires sacrifices of time and energy for his flock. We need to stay alert for opportunities to bless the men and women who minister in our churches. The same respect is due anyone who works to support a family or to help those outside the family. Just as an ox grazes as it labors, we don't begrudge people a good living; instead, we look for ways to bless those efforts.

God, show me ways to bless those who labor for you. Give me ideas that will delight the hearts of the people in my life who work hard.

Tatters Made Whole

"Max, down!" Allison grabbed her puppy's collar and banished the golden retriever to the kitchen.

"Sorry. He didn't ruin your nylons, did he?" she asked her guest.

"No, he's just an overgrown pup. We've had our share of dogs." Carol reached over the baby gate to pet Max on the head. "Golden retrievers are satisfying pets, once they are house-trained and get through the chewing stage."

Max wagged his tail and knocked the baby gate over in his enthusiasm for the affection.

"I hope you're right," Allison said as she repositioned the gate. "You can see this gate is more of a psychological barrier than a real one, if he really wants to explore. His chewing would cost us a fortune in ruined socks alone if we gave him the run of the house."

Leaving Max whining behind the gate, Carol followed Allison into the den and showed her the quilt squares she had brought along. "This is the fabric I need to match,"

Carol said, pointing to a dark blue material studded with tiny pink rosebuds. "When the quilt store gave me your name, the clerk said you had lots of old fabric."

"I think I can help you." Allison opened an ornate chest that decorated a corner of the room. "I remember when that material was very popular in the 1960s. Stores carried the design in every color imaginable."

"That's about when I started this quilt. Sure wish I'd thought to buy enough to finish the project. I didn't realize that five babies, in rapid succession, plus a sick mother and then a sick father, would delay my completing this quilt for twenty years."

Allison dug through the fabric scraps that filled her trunk. "Eureka!" She pulled out a length of cloth with a triumphant flourish. "I thought I remembered having some of this. I have it in brown tones, too, if you need that color."

"Wonderful!" Carol exclaimed, holding the two pieces together to prove the match. "What a big stash of fabric. I guess it proves you're a lifelong quilter."

"That quilt over there is what started me on my hobby," Allison said, pointing to a Baltimore Album quilt spread across the back of her sofa.

"What a beauty." Carol sat down for a closer look. "I think Baltimore Album quilts are the most showy, festive quilts of all."

"My grandmother made that one for my mother when she married. She cut all the red in the flowers and wreaths from her old Christmas tablecloths."

"I'll bet it took her a long time to stitch such elaborate designs," Carol said, fingering one square with a basket made of woven red strips and lavishly overflowing with colorful flowers.

"When I was a little girl, I remember Grandma telling me that sewing the quilt was a comfort to her. Granddaddy had died shortly before she began working on it."

"I think therapy is why I pulled out this old quilt project. I hope a creative project will help put behind me the injustice my husband's boss has done to him." With Allison's encouragement, Carol slowly unfolded her story. What began as a search for material grew into an afternoon of shared lives and interests, igniting a new friendship. Allison lingered on the front steps, saying good-bye to her new friend. Reluctant to stop the conversation, Carol left after fifteen more minutes elapsed.

When Allison stepped back into her house, she saw Max retreat into her den.

"Max, what are you doing out? Got a bad conscience? You should—jumping on my guest, knocking over the gate." She picked up the gate and leaned it against the wall before going into her den.

She stood in the doorway, stunned. "Maaax! You, you," Allison sputtered in outrage that rapidly disintegrated into tears. "You didn't," she blubbered. "You." She would have slapped the dog, but he slunk under the coffee table. In a heap on her den floor lay her grandmother's Baltimore Album quilt, a big hole chewed out of the center. Sobbing, she picked up saliva-dampened pieces.

She reached under the coffee table to grab Max by the collar and pull him out. "Bad dog! Bad, bad, horrid dog!" A long piece of material dangled from his mouth. She pried his mouth open and retrieved it, along with some other bits caught in his teeth. She put the soggy mess into a baggie, gathered up her damaged quilt, and headed to see her friend Billy Jean.

The tears were still running when she knocked at Billy Jean's door. With her years of experience putting treasured but tattered quilts back together, Billy Jean managed to calm her friend. She gingerly spread out the gooey pieces and surveyed the damage. "I can fix it," she announced.

"You can?" Allison looked incredulous.

"For a tidy sum I can. This is how I earn my living, you know."

"But I'm sure Max swallowed some. I couldn't rescue all the pieces."

"I have some matching reds and greens I can use," Billy Jean reassured Allison. "Since you and I go a long way back, I'll give you a bargain price."

Overwhelmed with gratitude that her heirloom could be restored, Allison would have paid the full price. "After it's fixed, I promise to hang it on the wall where Max can't get to it—if the miserable critter doesn't lose his happy home first."

"That's what doghouses are for," Billy Jean said and laughed, seeing the idea click with Allison.

The Master Pattern

The Spirit of the Sovereign LORD is on me,
because the LORD has anointed me
to preach good news to the poor.

191

He has sent me to bind up the brokenhearted,
    to proclaim freedom for the captives
    and release from darkness for the prisoners.

Isaiah 61:1

Billy Jean restores damaged quilts. Of much more significance, God restores people. Regardless of the holes and damage from our pasts, God is able to put us back together—more whole than ever before. When our hearts break, our Lord Jesus is ready to bring us comfort.

God, let me be an instrument of restoration in your hands. Make me a soothing ointment to the heartbroken.

A Cry for Help
and a Pierced Quilt

Ruth paced around and around the plank table her husband had built before the baby came. As long as she walked and patted the infant, Lori was quiet. The moment she tried to put the child in her cradle, the baby shrieked.

"Shush, little baby, don't you cry. Don't wake your pa," she whispered into the baby's ear. "He works hard and needs his sleep." She turned her words into a soft melody, singing with the hope of lulling the baby to sleep. "Be a good little girl, and Daddy will build us a rocking chair." Her tired legs made her hope he would get to it before harvesting the crops required all his time. For now, walking and bouncing seemed to be the key to quieting Lori.

She sang prayers as she paced, thanking God for a safe childbirth far from doctors on their Oklahoma homestead. She thanked the Lord for a healthy baby and prayed for her family's continued protection. She could at least put her sleepless nights to good use by talking to God, even in her tired state.

When the baby finally relaxed into sleep, Ruth carefully stretched out beside Jerome on top of the Baltimore Album quilt, keeping Lori close against her chest. Eventually, the exhausted mother successfully shifted the baby onto the bed between her and Jerome, and they all slept.

Ruth barely realized when Jerome slid out of bed and dressed. Before he left for his chores in the barn behind their log cabin, he leaned over and whispered, "The baby gave you a bad night. Try to get a little rest while she's quiet. I need to mend fences after I feed the livestock. Maybe little Lori will let you get a nice nap." Jerome smiled at their eight-week-old baby asleep in the middle of her parents' bed.

Ruth didn't know how much later it was or why she awoke. Terror confronted her the moment she opened her eyes. There, between her and Lori, lay a two-foot-long diamondback snake stretched out on the bed. It wasn't moving, just watching her and the baby.

Inch by inch, she eased out of bed. The snake stared. Keeping her eyes on the unmoving reptile, Ruth backed to the door. There she grasped a pitchfork. *Thank God,* she thought, *Jerome forgot to take this back to the barn this morning.* With an inward cry for help, Ruth raised the pitchfork above her head and brought it down swiftly, stabbing the snake. Dropping her grip on the farm tool, she snatched her baby away from the snake's last writhing twists. Lori cried from her abrupt awakening. Ruth cried from relief. Her cries brought Jerome running from the fence repair.

194

"I'm sorry, honey," Jerome said after he tossed the dead snake out the door. He held up the Baltimore Album quilt to show his wife three holes pierced by the pitchfork and red stains from the snake's blood.

Ruth cuddled her baby close to her heart. "I'll mend it. Even an heirloom from our more civilized existence in Baltimore is nothing compared to our precious child."

Jerome cupped his hand behind the baby's head. "Let's give thanks."

The Master Pattern

If you make the Most High your dwelling—
    even the LORD, who is my refuge—
then no harm will befall you,
    no disaster will come near your tent.
For he will command his angels concerning you
    to guard you in all your ways.

Psalm 91:9–11

God is always near. Many times he protects us from evil we don't even know is present. To make God our refuge, we keep our thoughts and minds focused on our Lord. We dwell on the goodness of God. We determine to live our lives in constant awareness of him. We draw close to God in prayer and in studying the Bible. While we probably won't hear the flapping of wings, and only in rare instances do people actually see angels, they are present to guard us.

Thank you, God, for your protection over my life and the lives of those I love. Help me to dwell in your presence and take refuge in your love and character whenever my heart troubles me.

A Tiny Baby and a Big Prayer

"Guess what I found out the day before we flew out of the States?" Olivia asked, hanging a shirt from her suitcase in her hotel room closet.

"Tell me. I'm never good with guesses," responded Barb as she unpacked alongside her roommate for the ten-day mission trip high in the mountains of Peru.

"I'm pregnant. Good thing I'd already paid the fees for this dental mission, or my husband would have canceled the trip."

"What about morning sickness?" Barb asked.

"Our trip is short enough that I think I'll be home before I run into any problem with nausea."

In spite of the altitude, heat, and new pregnancy, Olivia cleaned teeth and dispensed dental floss without any problems. Everyone on the medical mission found he or she tired more easily in the high altitude, but all of them worked long days anyway. Each morning people lined up, seeking free dental care they couldn't otherwise obtain. No one wanted to leave a need unmet.

"I'm so glad I came," Olivia said as she sat under a tree, taking a short break on the last day of the clinic. "I love these Peruvian people."

"Me, too." Barb perched on a stump a short distance away. "I've met a lot of people hungry to know more about God. Why don't you rest a while longer?" she said to Olivia, who looked at her watch and started to get up. "We leave for our plane before long."

Olivia leaned against the tree trunk. "Okay. I'm all packed and ready to go, as soon as we close the clinic."

By the time the dental mission team boarded its airplane, Olivia was scratching. "Some dastardly insect must have munched on me while I sat on the ground before we left."

Barb had some calamine lotion in her purse and gave it to Olivia to apply to her legs. By the time they arrived in the United States, she'd emptied the bottle, rubbing it on both arms, her face, and as far down the neck of her blouse as she could reach without disrobing.

"You see a doctor first thing, Olivia, and call me with a report," Barb ordered. Her forehead wrinkled in worry as she hugged her friend good-bye at the airport. She then flew on to her home in another state.

Olivia's husband, James, was the one who called. "They've admitted Olivia to the hospital. Her face and whole body are swollen."

"What on earth happened?" Barb asked, frowning.

"The doctors think she's had an allergic reaction to some kind of insect bite. The physicians have put her on steroids, but she's worried the medicine will harm our baby. The medical team is more concerned she might have a disease that would damage the baby's development." James's words wavered and stopped.

"I'll pray." Barb began to intercede for her friends over the phone line.

"Thanks, Barb," James said when she finished. "Don't stop praying. I'll tell Olivia." The line went dead, and Barb kept on praying, wishing for some way to express her love.

Of course, she thought. She would make a Baltimore Album quilt with squares depicting mountains, waterfalls, and other significant scenes from their Peruvian trip. The bright colors of a Baltimore Album quilt were appropriate for a blanket commemorating Peru.

"It takes nine months for a baby to be born. I'll try to finish Olivia's quilt before she gives birth," Barb told her husband. She prayed for the health and destiny of the unborn child while she cut, appliquéd, and quilted her gift.

She'd nearly finished the project when James called to tell her William was born. "He's perfectly healthy. There's not a thing wrong with him, and Olivia's fine."

Barb held the phone away from her ear. James was shouting his joy.

She tenderly wrapped the quilt and mailed it with a note about the significance of each square. "A quilt to remember William's first trip," Barb wrote. After all, he had traveled to Peru in Olivia's womb, even if he hadn't seen the country. "I prayed every day for your baby while I stitched. I covered him with prayer, as you will cover William with this quilt."

The Master Pattern

Therefore confess your sins to each other and pray for each other so that you may be healed. The prayer of a righteous man is powerful and effective.

James 5:16

Prayer is a privilege God grants to us. While we live on this earth, we probably will not completely comprehend the power of prayer. When we arrive in heaven, we may be surprised to discover the results of our fleeting, as well as our earnest and long-rendered, prayers.

When we accept Jesus as Savior, he bestows his righteousness on us, and our prayers are effective. The potency of our prayers does not depend on how we feel, on how polished our wording is, on how lengthily or frequently we pray, or on how well we succeed in our day-to-day living. Our effectiveness in prayer is the result of the righteousness of Christ, which he bestows on his beloved followers.

Thank you, God, for granting me the righteousness of Christ when I came to you believing. Help me to pray faithfully, according to your leading.

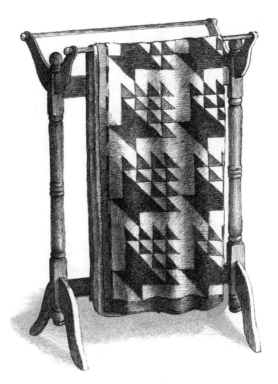

Grandmother's Flower Basket

If ever a quilt blanketed folks with comfort, this one—dating back to 1830—did. Grandmother's Flower Basket became a favorite during the Civil War for both Northern and Southern women trying to raise funds for hospital supplies and gunboats; the Women's Christian Temperance Society also used this pattern for quilt sales aimed at funding lobbies for child-labor laws. Much of the pattern's popularity for such sales came from its artful piecing of triangles to form the basket and its inventive appliqué of the handle and flowers. Whether these quilts were splashed with a wide range of colors or limited to two or three, the effect was pleasing.

Careful coordination of fabric colors, shapes, and sizes mean the difference between a glorious Grandmother's Flower Basket quilt and a disastrous pile of mismatched pieces. In the stories that follow, humility, devotion, relentless prayers, and an amazing invention showcase people's frailty and God's faithfulness—the beautiful thread that makes the quilts of our lives gorgeous, graceful, and complete.

Messy Stitches, Real Friends

"Lola! I'm glad you could make it." Hannah held the door open for her recently widowed neighbor, who lived on the next farm three miles of golden wheat fields away.

"I wouldn't miss a quilting bee for anything. It gets mighty lonely since Amy moved away with her new husband. The evenings are so long, I find myself sitting on the porch and talking to the wheat," Lola replied. Her misty eyes betrayed the smile on her lips.

"We love having you come, don't we?" Hannah's firm nod to the ladies already gathered around the quilting frame brought the desired murmur of welcome.

"Come sit by me," Bertha said, moving over on the bench. "Help me piece the pinks in this Grandmother's Flower Basket."

Wasting no time, Lola soon had her needle flashing in and out of the floral fabric as she eagerly sought the latest news of the farming community.

Bertha bit her lips to avoid commenting about the importance of matching the pieces and sewing small stitches.

"I hope that when we finish this Grandmother's Flower Basket quilt for Hannah's daughter, we will be expecting so many new babies that we'll have lots of reasons to hold quilting bees," Lola said with a sigh. "I don't know what I'd do without the chance to get off my lonely hill and come to sew. You can't imagine how dark night feels without my Ben. Then Amy married . . ." Lola dabbed her eyes.

Hannah exchanged a smile with Grace. "This is as good a time as any to make your announcement."

Grace blushed. "Looks as if a baby quilt will be in order. Around the time for spring planting, John and I will be having a baby."

After the group offered Grace surprised congratulations, Bertha added, "And I heard the Meyers are expecting."

"From the long gazes Bart Smith is casting at your Rosy, Bertha, we may have another wedding quilt to put together," Hannah said, smiling at her friend.

"If we can overlook his table manners." Bertha's voice was so low, only Lola heard her.

"Such an industrious young man. He'll make you proud someday," Lola said and patted Bertha's hand. "His cleft chin isn't hard to look at either."

"That's what Rosy thinks." Bertha squared her shoulders. "I guess we all remember our starry-eyed courting days."

"How long was it before we saw falling stars instead? Eventually two personalities collide," Hannah noted to wry laughter.

"But love kept us adjusting. Wish I had Ben's snoring to adjust to now." Lola kept raising her eyes from the work to visit with the women, all the while keeping her needle working. Still, she was the first to get up when the sun's shadows lengthened in the afternoon. "I'd best go. No one else to do the chores."

"I'd like to drop by your house, Lola, for tea next week. I'll bring some pumpkin biscuits to go with it," Hannah said as she helped her with her coat.

"I'd love the company." Lola's face brightened.

The ladies sat, needles still, until Lola's wagon pulled away.

"Okay, ladies. What do we need to fix today?" Hannah asked.

"None of these pink pieces fit together properly. See how the basket looks crooked? And her appliqué stitches show." Bertha sighed and passed around several pairs of scissors. The women began to snip away Lola's work.

"If she'd look at her sewing more than us while she talks, maybe she'd do better work," Hannah commented.

"I'm still glad she comes," Bertha said. "Filling one day a month with a little joy for Lola is more important than a perfect quilt."

"Anyway, it's perfect by the time you kind ladies redo it," Grace added, as she repositioned one of the misplaced pink triangles.

"I'm relieved she never seems to notice the difference the next time she sees the quilt."

"I'll admit I'm glad she feels she must leave early," Hannah said. "Gives us a chance to fix up her work without hurting her feelings."

The Master Pattern

Beloved, let us love one another: for love is of God; and every one that loveth is born of God, and knoweth God. He that loveth not knoweth not God; for God is love.

1 John 4:7–8 KJV

All of us do imperfect work at one time or another. By overlooking our irritation and focusing on each other's successes instead, we spread God's love and give the blessing of acceptance to one another. And acceptance fosters change better than criticism.

God, help me to see others through your eyes of love. Keep my focus on how to bless, not correct, the people in my life.

The Ugliest Fabric Contest

"Is this hideous enough?" Brandie held up a bundle of purple fabric with large yellow polka dots.

"I'd say it's a winner," Shelby answered, wrinkling her nose.

"Someone had a bad dream when he or she designed this cloth," Brandie said as she pointed to a teal material with what looked like brown picture frames at crazy angles, dodging purple and orange flowers.

"Keep your voice down. I don't think the clerk at the last stall appreciated your calling some of her fabric ugly."

The two women roamed the booths of fabric vendors at the Paducah, Kentucky, quilt festival. Their goal was the opposite of the usual shoppers in the room full of vendors' cubicles. Instead of looking for material that appealed to them, they were trying to find the most horrid fabric for a contest among their friends.

"Fran said she bought her ugly material at home before flying to meet us in Paducah, but she wouldn't give me a hint about how it looks," Brandie said.

"Here's a good candidate." Shelby giggled and pointed to a bolt of orange half-moons splashed with yellow zigzags on a bright chartreuse background.

"Pretty bad, but I want to look around some more before I make up my mind," Brandie said. "I want to win this contest."

"You'll get no competition from me," Shelby said as she picked up a bolt of blue material covered with red bows. "No one would think this is a monstrosity. I'll take an eighth of a yard." She held it out to the clerk. "I think making a quilt from all the ugly material we bring is a bit more of a challenge than I want."

"I'm going all out, because I can't bear for Agatha to win again. Last year she was so proud of the quilt she made out of all our ugly prints, it made me sick. Insufferable is what she was. Still is. Brag, brag, brag about anything or everything." Brandie put her hand on her hip. With her other hand in the air she swaggered in front of the vendor's counter. "I'm going to win and make the ugly quilt this year."

"So you can be the one to brag?" Shelby raised an eyebrow.

"Oh, you," Brandie said and stuck out her tongue. "That's not my style."

Shelby turned serious. "I think Agatha boasts because she has an enormous need to feel as if she's okay, to try to convince us she's special. To me, she seems sad and insecure."

"You're probably right, but I still intend to win the contest. Here's a good one." Brandie spread out a fabric of yellow stripes covered with lime-green dots, which alternated with red stripes dissected by lines of the same green. "I get dizzy just looking at this print. I'll buy it."

When the quilting friends gathered in the lobby of the hotel they were staying in, they laid their finds on a table. The coordinator of the contest assigned each woman's material a number, so none of the ladies knew whose cloth she was voting most ugly. With lots of laughter, the women cast their votes. Brandie won, with her red and yellow stripes. Agatha's pattern of large electric lightbulbs came in second.

At home, Brandie decided a Grandmother's Flower Basket pattern was a good one to use. She could get by with incorporating only small pieces of some of the more objectionable designs in a flower petal or woven into a basket.

She studied each piece, trying to find something good in it, looking for a pretty spot of color or motif. She turned over some patterned green fabrics to use the backs; she cut these into leaves for the flowers in the quilt. The muted backsides provided a nice variety of shades. The large yellow polka dots from one swatch made good centers for the flowers. Her own material with red stripes decorated her baskets like a ribbon, and Shelby's bows gave a finishing touch.

Whenever Brandie set her mind to discover a way to utilize a material she thought hopeless, she surprised herself with her ideas. She even dyed some pieces in a tea bath, which muted the colors and made them prettier.

By the time she finished her quilt, Brandie saw both ugly fabrics and her friend Agatha in a new light. If Brandie sought ways that even the worst fabrics could fit into the pattern, she easily found creative and pleasing uses for them. In the same way, if she looked for what Agatha contributed through her skill at quilting, she could appreciate the woman. If she examined what lay behind Agatha's insecurities, Brandie developed compassion born of understanding.

Delighted with her finished Grandmother's Flower Basket quilt, she scolded herself: "Remember, no bragging."

The Master Pattern

Therefore, if anyone is in Christ, he is a new creation; the old has gone, the new has come!

2 Corinthians 5:17

To Brandie's surprise, when she searched for the best aspects of the homely material, she found ways to use it attractively. Sometimes, simply changing the angle from which she viewed the piece helped her stop seeing it as ugly but instead as holding interesting possibilities. Brandie discovered the same was true about her friend Agatha. So may we all.

Help me to see the new creature you are creating in each one of your people. Give me the angle from which you want me to see others and the ability to appreciate them.

A Prayer with Every Stitch

"She's going to die." Alissa's wrenching words reached Estelle before she entered the door of her daughter's hospital room.

There, Estelle found Alissa sobbing in her husband's arms. Bert climbed up on the hospital bed to hold his wife closer. "Dr. Barnes says our baby was born with Beta Strep and will probably die," he explained to his mother-in-law. "He says this is a potent virus that attacks the baby's breathing system."

Estelle rushed to her daughter, and the three clung together.

"Let's go to Jesus about the baby," Estelle said and led the stunned new parents in prayer.

Between renewed hope based on prayer and emotional exhaustion, the distraught family quieted.

"We haven't named her yet," Bert said.

"Let's call her Hope. I have hope since we prayed," said Alissa, drying her eyes on Bert's shirt.

As days passed, the news from the hospital staff worsened. "Her lungs may collapse, and her heart may stop," Dr. Barnes solemnly told the young parents. "She needs to go to Charlottesville, Virginia, where they have a more sophisticated machine than our rural hospital does."

"So far away," Alissa murmured as she clutched Bert's hand.

"And time is important," Dr. Barnes added. "I don't think she could survive the trip if we tried to fly her. We'll send her by ambulance. I'll order the ambulance equipped with special breathing equipment for infants. But I warn you: It will be a delicate procedure to move her while her lungs are in such a precarious condition. We need to give the antibiotics some time to start working before we begin the transfer."

As the family waited, Estelle stood at the neonatal intensive care window. She watched a nurse ring a bell for assistance and begin squeezing a bag positioned over Hope's face. Other staff members came running in and clustered around the small bassinet.

When Bert wheeled Alissa up to the window to view their baby, she asked, "Why are so many nurses there? What are they doing with that bag?"

Should I say the purpose is to force air into Hope's lungs? wondered Estelle. Instead, she prayed silently.

"I can't watch." Alissa lowered her face into her hands, and Bert wheeled her back to her room.

When Estelle joined them a while later, her daughter raised an anguished face. "My doctor says I'll have to wait until tomorrow to travel to Charlottesville, so I can't ride in the ambulance with the baby. Bert needs to stay here in order to drive me up."

"I'll go," Estelle said. "Since I'm retired, I can stay until you come, and longer if need be. Maybe you'd like me around while you regain strength from childbirth."

Estelle hurried home to pack a suitcase, unsure how many days or weeks she would be away. Then she quickly rummaged through her fabric stash and pulled out pastel-colored prints. She loaded a tote with quilting supplies.

Back at the hospital, a soft-spoken chaplain asked, "Do you want last rites administered?"

Instead of answering, Bert took the chaplain's hand, made a circle with Alissa and Estelle, and cried out to God to heal Hope.

Dr. Barnes supervised the transfer of the baby, stroking his chin as he watched. He looked Alissa in the eye and said quietly, "Prepare yourself. Even if the child survives the trip, chances are she won't live more than four months."

Seated beside the driver, Estelle prayed for her little granddaughter as each mile passed.

An efficient team met the ambulance, and Estelle continued her prayers in the waiting room.

Later, a nurse stopped to encourage Estelle. "Good news!" she said. "We managed to get the baby on a ventilator and didn't need the heart-lung machine after all."

Yet for every encouraging sign of progress the hours brought, doctors offered distressing speculations piled upon dire predictions. To cope, Estelle began what she thought of as Hope's miracle quilt. She cut mauve and pink gingham triangles to make the baskets for the Grandmother's Flower Basket pattern. By the time Bert and Alissa arrived late the next day, she'd cut enough flower petals of delicate colors to fill the baskets with a profusion of cloth blooms. With every stitch on the quilt, Estelle cried to the Lord to spare her granddaughter.

Eighteen days later, Dr. Moore shook his head in amazement. "I can't believe the rapid recovery. Hope is doing so well, she can go home. She may have a slow start, but she will catch up and be just fine."

By the time Hope was pulling herself up on furniture and taking tentative steps, Estelle had finished the miracle quilt—a symbol of her love and in memory of her prayers.

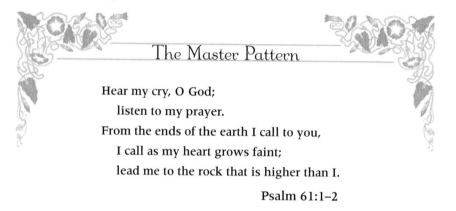

The Master Pattern

Hear my cry, O God;
     listen to my prayer.
From the ends of the earth I call to you,
     I call as my heart grows faint;
     lead me to the rock that is higher than I.

Psalm 61:1–2

God cares about what troubles us, whether our concerns are life threatening, like the illness Hope battled, or other types of problems such as relationships or finances. He sees and understands our heartaches and is willing and able to help us with them. God hears our cries. He will bring peace to our hearts and solutions to our problems when we bring our painful circumstances to him.

I bring the troubles of my life to you, God. Send your peace into each situation, and heal my wounded soul.

A New Pattern for Life

"Louisa, you must get busy on your quilt dowry," Della said as she rocked her feverish five-year-old near the fireplace. "How do you expect to turn Flint's head without a dozen quilts for your hope chest? He's a handsome young man with a lot of admirers."

"Mother! I can't believe you're thinking about dowries when Violet is so sick." Louisa tried to stifle a smile as she stirred the gruel on the stove.

"I had plenty of time to think while I stayed up half the night with your sick sister. Better to think of weddings and happiness for my daughter than to worry about all the burdens of today."

"Let me take a turn tending Violet." Louisa dipped a rag in a bucket of water, lay it over her sister's flushed forehead, and picked her up. "I haven't had time for quilting, Mother. Our other sewing needs never seem to come to an end." She settled into the rocking chair with Violet while Della stretched, then rubbed the small of her back with her fists.

"Just yesterday Adam tore his overalls and a shirt," Louisa said with a sigh. "I hate mending heavy denim."

Della smiled. "Can't fault an eight-year-old's enthusiasm to help his pa fix fences."

"Fixing and climbing are two different things," Louisa murmured, rocking Violet.

Della stuck to her subject. "Look at your competition. Ivy nearly made herself dizzy batting her eyes at Flint during church cleaning day this spring. Which reminds me, the seed is here for our spring garden, and in a week or two, the moon will be right for planting." She took over stirring the pot of gruel.

"See, there is always some pressing chore to do. If the proper number of quilts is the criteria for winning Flint, it's hopeless." Louisa rocked faster. "As if we don't have enough to do, next week Grandma's coming to live here. No doubt, she'll be needing us to sew new clothes."

"She can't see to sew her own," Della said, setting the pot of breakfast gruel on the warmer. She picked up her mending basket while she waited for the family males to return from their chores in the barn.

"I have a better chance of winning Flint's attention with my cherry cobbler. If sewing is a requirement, I'll be an old maid. Nightgowns stitched for Grandma aren't likely to make Flint want to come courting."

"I'll bet he'd settle for a smile and the sparkle of your brown eyes," commented Roscoe, Louisa's father, who was carrying a bucket of milk into the house. Adam followed. "What you need, daughter, is an Iron Needle Woman."

"You mean one of those new sewing machines?" Louisa asked.

"Grandma had a friend with a machine a long time ago," Della remembered. "Spent a fortune on it, cantankerous gadget. She finally gave up sewing with it and used it as a stand in the window for her indoor herb garden."

"Ah, that was before 1854, when Mr. Singer improved Mr. Howe's invention. The machines work right well now." Roscoe leaned over and laid his hand on Violet's head. "She feels cooler."

"We can't afford such a luxury," Louisa said, smiling at Violet, who opened her eyes.

"Your Aunt Lily told me how she bought one this spring," Roscoe said. He picked up Violet and swung her in his arms. She laughed.

"Lily always had spendthrift ways," Della responded. "She's no better off than the rest of us in this valley, wresting food out of rock-strewn fields and bartering with wood from our forests." She finished sewing on a button and bit off the thread with her teeth.

"Lily said that Mr. Singer offers a deal to buy his sewing machines over time," Roscoe said. "She paid five dollars down. Now she pays Mr. Hughlett, at the general store, three dollars a month until she pays off the one-hundred-dollar price." He handed Violet to Della. "Feel her forehead. Her fever's broken."

"Reckless purchase, if you ask me. Why, it'd take almost three years of coming up with that payment every month to make a whole hundred dollars." Della set Violet in a chair by the table. "Feeling better, sweetheart? I'll spoon up some gruel to give you strength."

Roscoe sat beside Violet. "Paying by the month, you have your machine right away to zip through your sewing. And you can earn the three dollars by selling the things you make."

Louisa's eyes sparkled. "I could make and sell quilts to the other families around here. No one has time to stitch all the things they need. I'll wager I could earn money fast enough to pay off the machine. I could even sew curtains for the room Pa's adding for Grandma Fran."

"I don't know," Della said. "Grandma's care is going to take a lot of work. She can't move around without help." She set bowls of gruel in front of the rest of the family.

"I wish God would help us with difficulties," Louisa said.

"He does. He gives us strength to do what's needed. He makes our burdens lighter. Look at Violet," Roscoe said. He hugged the child eating gruel beside him. "She's on the mend. That's one burden lifted. God gives us the tools to lift our spirits, his Word to study, mouths to praise him, and spirits to sense his presence. I'm glad he also inspires men to design tools of wood and metal to make our work easier."

Before 1876 was over, Louisa had made and sold several quilts, aprons, bonnets, and nightgowns. She used the sewing machine to sew triangles together for lovely baskets for Grandmother's Flower Basket quilts, and then she devised a pattern to use machine-sewn triangles for stylized flowers to fill the baskets.

"Look at you, sewing away," Roscoe remarked, stopping to admire Louisa's work. Soon she was turning out a number of different quilt patterns with the machine. She hung the quilts on the fence by the road and had no trouble making her payment on the machine every month.

One day, some months later, Flint made his usual stop when he passed Louisa's house. He had fallen into a habit of visiting her each time he drove his wagon of grain to the mill. "I see you finished another quilt top," he remarked.

"Do you like it?" Louisa asked.

"I like the hands that made it." Flint reached out and took her hand.

Louisa blushed.

The Master Pattern

For my yoke is easy and my burden is light.

Matthew 11:30

By 1876, the Singer sewing machine was enjoying sales of several hundred thousand a year. The tool transformed the task of sewing for a family, lightening women's sewing burdens. God will supply us with the tools we need to handle all the tasks and troubles of our lives. Whether the tool is a physical item, such as the sewing machine, or a helpful mental outlook, our relationship with God helps us approach life joyfully.

Thank you for lifting my burdens and providing me with the tools to grow in my relationship with you.

Acknowledgments

I want to thank all the gracious people who shared their stories about quilts with me.

I'd especially like to thank Nancy Gloss, owner of Nancy's Calico Patch, and Mary Frances Ballard, Phyllis Porter, and Karen DiMarino, all of whom patiently answered my questions and supplied resources for my research.

I'm also grateful to my son Andrew, who gave his time and skill to critique this book.

A special thank-you to the prayer warriors who regularly lift my writing efforts to God.

About the Author

Mary Tatem loves quilting, but she doesn't come from a long line of quilters. She jokes that she made her first stitches on clumsily fashioned doll clothes. The first quilt she completed, after learning the art from a women's group, was for her daughter's wedding twenty-two years ago. She's been quilting ever since and has completed a number of Sunbonnet quilts for her grandchildren.

She does come from a long line of women skilled in textile arts. As a child, Mary carded wool for her grand-mother, who made simple quilts by sewing two sheets of white muslin together and using homegrown, carded wool for the middle layer. Yarn, sewn through all the layers at intervals and tied with knots, held the three layers in place. Mary remembers sleeping under those warm covers throughout childhood.

When not quilting—or writing about it—Mary hosts a bi-weekly home Bible study, works with her church's singles groups, and provides premarital counseling. She's been a

Sunday school teacher, a Girl Scout leader, and a sponsor for mothers' groups. She speaks on relationships and how to grow spiritually, and she leads writing workshops.

Mary has published three other books, including the best-selling *The Quilt of Life: A Patchwork of Devotional Thoughts.* Her feature articles have appeared in a variety of magazines.

Mary lives in Newport News, Virginia, with her husband; they have four adult children and fifteen grandchildren, who all love beautiful threads.

Visit the author's web site at www.marytatem.com.

About the Illustrator

Kevin Ingram, a professional illustrator and graphic artist in Grand Rapids, Michigan, works in a wide range of media, from oil to computer-aided design. Now at work on his own publishing project, he specializes in portraiture and freelance work for the publishing industry.

While he's never put needle to a quilting square, Kevin is keeper of a family quilt story: "My great-grandmother Maggie met with a group of ladies at a quilting guild in a rural Indiana church. Every week, around large quilting frames, they sewed and shared 'community news' (yes, gossip). After a few hours, they would pack up their needles and thread, stow the frames, and go their separate ways. All except Maggie. Because one of her friends in the guild was truly horrible at stitching, and Maggie knew the woman's work would never hold, she stayed behind to rip out all of her friend's work and restitch the squares. Maggie would never embarrass her friend, and none of the other women ever found out her quirky secret."

One of Maggie's quilts is depicted in an illustration for this book.

For more of Ingram's work, check out his website at www.kiarts.net.